The Mocktail Bar Guide

200 Recipes for Alcohol-Free Drinks

Frank Thomas & Karen L. Brown

Royalties from the sale of
this book support

MADD

 Meadowbrook Press
Distributed by Simon & Schuster
New York

Library of Congress Cataloging-in-Publication Data
Thomas, Frank, 1948-
    The mocktail bar guide / Frank Thomas & Karen Lancaster Brown.
        p. cm.
    Includes index.
    ISBN 0-88166-394-8 (Meadowbrook) ISBN 0-743-22345-4
    (Simon & Schuster)
        1. Non-alcoholic beverages. 2. Cocktails. I. Brown, Karen
    Lancaster, 1952 Feb. 19- II. Title.

    TX815 .T54 2001
    641.8'75—dc21   2001030290

Editorial Director: Christine Zuchora-Walske
Editors: Megan McGinnis, Angela Wiechmann
Production Manager: Paul Woods
Desktop Publishing: Danielle White
Cover Art: Doug Oudekerk
Index: Beverlee Day

© 2001 by Meadowbrook Creations

Published by Meadowbrook Press, 5451 Smetana Drive, Minnetonka,
Minnesota 55343

www.meadowbrookpress.com

BOOK TRADE DISTRIBUTION by Simon & Schuster, a division
of Simon and Schuster, Inc., 1230 Avenue of the Americas, New
York, New York 10020

05 04 03 02   10 9 8 7 6 5 4 3

Printed in the United States of America

Contents

Foreword iv

Introduction v

The Essentials v

Barware v

Glassware vi

Basic Ingredients viii

Garnishes viii

Mixology x

Liquid Measurements xi

Mocktails 1

Drinks for All Seasons 29

Winter 30

Winter Holidays 38

Spring 46

Spring Holidays 56

Summer 62

Summer Holidays 75

Fall 79

Fall Holidays 88

Sweet Endings 95

Coffees 96

Teas 101

Shakes & Floats 106

Index 111

Foreword

Parties are times for celebration, but all too often drunk driving turns these happy occasions into tragedies. By providing nonalcoholic drinks for designated drivers and those who don't want alcohol, hosts can help friends and family stay safe.

When planning an event, include the delicious mocktails and creative nonalcoholic beverages found in *The Mocktail Bar Guide* to provide guests with refreshing alternatives to alcoholic drinks. But if you're serving alcohol, remember these safety tips:

- Ask guests to appoint designated driver(s).
- Never serve alcohol to anyone under the legal drinking age (twenty-one), and never have youth serve alcohol.
- Appoint a reliable "bartender" to help keep track of the amount of alcohol guests consume.
- Prepare plenty of food so guests won't drink alcohol on empty stomachs; don't push alcoholic drinks.
- Provide entertainment or group activities.
- If guests drink alcohol, arrange a ride with a sober driver, call a taxi, or invite them to stay over.

We hope you'll enjoy this collection of great-tasting, nonalcoholic drink recipes, and we thank you for your support in making our roadways safer for our friends and families. For more information, please visit our web site at www.madd.org.

Millie I. Webb

Millie I. Webb
National President 2000–2002
Mothers Against Drunk Driving

Introduction

Whether you're hosting a back yard barbecue or an elegant buffet, it's always helpful to have a bar complete with the right equipment and ingredients.

The Essentials

Barware

Depending on the type of drinks you're serving, you'll need to have some of the following equipment on hand.

- Blender
- Cocktail shaker
- Strainer
- Measuring cups and spoons
- Mixing spoons and stirrers
- Paring knife and cutting board
- Vegetable peeler and zester
- Mixing glass
- Ice bucket and tongs
- Toothpicks (for garnishes)
- Cocktail napkins and coasters

Glassware

Presentation is everything. A stylish glass makes for a more satisfying sipper. Make sure you have the right glasses for your offerings.

Highball **Collins** **Old-fashioned**

Red wineglass **White wineglass** **Champagne flute**

Tulip glass **Irish coffee glass** **Coffee mug**

Brandy snifter

Balloon

Demitasse

Teacup

Hurricane

Parfait

Cocktail

Beer mug

Pilsner

Margarita

Daiquiri

Punch bowl

Basic Ingredients

If you have the following basic ingredients on hand, you'll be able to make many of the tantalizing treats in this book any time you want.

- Club soda
- Ginger ale
- Cola and lemon–lime soda
- Sparkling water
- Seltzer
- Fruit juices
- Vegetable juice
- Frozen fruits
- Vanilla ice cream
- Chocolate syrup
- Coffees and teas
- Grenadine
- Salt
- Sugar
- Lemon and lime juices
- Cream and milk
- Vanilla extract
- Tabasco and Worcestershire sauces

Garnishes

Put some pizzazz into your drinks with these finishing touches.

- Fruit twists, wedges, and slices (See the instructions on the next page.)

- Maraschino cherries
- Whipped cream
- Chocolate shavings and sprinkles
- Celery stalks
- Mint leaves or sprigs
- Cinnamon sticks
- Margarita salt and colored sugar (See the instructions below.)
- Ground nutmeg
- Ground cinnamon

Twists: Use a paring knife or vegetable peeler to remove a long, thin section of a lemon or lime peel. Rub the strip around the glass rim, then twist a small drop of oil from the strip into the drink. Drop the strip into the drink as a garnish.

Wedges: Cut the fruit in half from top to bottom, then slice it into wedges. Remove pith and seeds if desired. Cut each wedge to fit on the glass rim.

Slices: Cut the fruit into round, thin slices. Remove seeds if desired. Float a slice on top of the drink or cut halfway across each slice and insert it on the glass rim.

Salted or sugared glass rims: Pour salt or sugar into a small saucer. Rub the glass rim with a lemon, lime, or water, then press the rim into the salt or sugar and twirl it until it's coated.

Mixology

- Each recipe yields one serving unless otherwise noted. Recipes can be doubled or tripled, although the drinks will taste best if made one at a time.

- Unless otherwise noted, *ice* means *ice cubes*. To make cracked ice, place ice cubes in a large plastic bag, lay a towel over the bag, and strike the bag with a wooden mallet to break the cubes into jagged chunks. Cracked ice can be used instead of ice cubes in mixed drinks for a different presentation. To make crushed ice, follow the same procedure for making cracked ice except strike the bag until the cubes are nearly pulverized. For added fun, use decorative ice cubes. To make these, half-fill ice cube trays with water and drop a chunk of brightly colored fruit or mint leaves into each section. Top off with water and freeze.

- To achieve the best taste and texture, make sure the ingredients are fresh if a recipe specifies fresh ingredients. Also, make sure ingredients are at the temperature indicated in the recipe; for example, *cold* or *chilled* means the ingredients are at refrigerator temperature and *ice-cold* means the ingredients are near 32°F or 0°C.

- All extracts and syrups required in the following recipes are nonalcoholic.

Liquid Measurements

1 gallon = 4 quarts = 8 pints = 16 cups = 128 fluid ounces

½ gallon = 2 quarts = 4 pints = 8 cups = 64 fluid ounces

¼ gallon = 1 quart = 2 pints = 4 cups = 32 fluid ounces

½ quart = 1 pint = 2 cups = 16 fluid ounces

¼ quart = ½ pint = 1 cup = 8 fluid ounces

¾ cup = 6 fluid ounces = 12 tablespoons = 36 teaspoons

½ cup = 4 fluid ounces = 8 tablespoons = 24 teaspoons

¼ cup = 2 fluid ounces = 4 tablespoons = 12 teaspoons

⅛ cup = 1 fluid ounce = 2 tablespoons = 6 teaspoons

Mocktails

*Recipes for delicious, alcohol-free variations
of over fifty popular cocktails*

Black Russian

Romance a new sweetie or reconnect with your long-time love over this sophisticated sipper that tops a wonderful evening.

4 ounces cold half-and-half
2 tablespoons chocolate syrup
Crushed ice

Pour first 2 ingredients over ice in shaker and shake well. Strain over crushed ice in old-fashioned glass.

Blarney Stone

Rave reviews will be your reward with the sweet-and-tart Blarney Stone. It's just the right mate for outdoor grilling or indoor lunching.

5 ounces pineapple juice
1 ounce grenadine
Maraschino cherry

Pour first 2 ingredients over ice in old-fashioned glass. Garnish with maraschino cherry.

Blood & Sand

Grenadine adds sweetness and color to this fruity fave. It's a combination of flavors that will make you come back for more.

4 ounces orange juice
2 ounces pineapple juice
1 ounce grenadine
Maraschino cherry

Pour first 3 ingredients over ice in highball glass and stir. Garnish with maraschino cherry.

Bloody Mary

Savor the good things in life: brunch with your best friend and a delicious bloody mary. The mixture of spices adds zip and zest.

12 ounces cold tomato juice
⅛ teaspoon celery salt
2 pinches of white pepper
½ teaspoon fresh horseradish
1 fresh garlic clove, minced
¼ cup chopped fresh onion
Pinch of fresh parsley
Green margarita salt
Celery stalk with leaves

Purée first 7 ingredients in blender at high speed 30 seconds. Wet rim of collins glass, then coat with green salt. Carefully pour mixture into glass and add celery stalk. Serve immediately.

Bocci Ball

Exotic, elegant, and oh-so easy to make. A hint of almond flavoring turns orange juice into a thing to be treasured. Serve up with biscotti at brunch.

1 ounce almond syrup
7 ounces orange juice

Pour ingredients over ice in highball glass and stir.

Brandy Alexander

Relax after dinner with this seductive sipper. A hint of nutmeg sets it apart.

4 ounces cold half-and-half
1½ tablespoons chocolate syrup
Pinch of ground nutmeg

Pour first 2 ingredients over ice in shaker and shake vigorously 10–15 seconds. Pour all contents into old-fashioned glass and dust top with ground nutmeg.

Cape Codder

Named for the beautiful New England coast and all its luscious cranberries, this brisk and breezy beverage is enjoyed by people from all regions.

6 ounces cranberry juice
½ ounce lime juice
Lime wedge

Pour juices over ice in old-fashioned glass and stir. Garnish rim with lime wedge.

Cherry Gimlet

Our version of this classic will remind you of simpler times. There's nothing simple about the taste, though. It's absolutely divine.

½ ounce grenadine
¼ ounce lime juice
4 ounces lemon-lime soda
Maraschino cherry

Pour first 3 ingredients over ice in shaker. Shake 5 seconds. Pour into old-fashioned glass and add maraschino cherry.

Chi Chi

Sweet coconut cream adds an exotic air to this potion. Top with a festive flower and serve in a coconut shell if you're really ambitious.

8 ounces pineapple juice
2 ounces cream of coconut
Maraschino cherry
Pineapple wedge

Pour first 2 ingredients over ice in collins glass and stir. Spear last 2 ingredients with toothpick and add to drink.

Citrus Collins

There are as many versions of the collins as there are personalities in your crowd. Serve this one to your adventurous pals—it's a trip.

6 ounces fresh grapefruit juice, chilled
½ ounce red currant syrup
¼ ounce lemon juice
Cracked ice
Half an orange slice

Pour first 4 ingredients into shaker and shake vigorously 15 seconds. Pour all contents into collins glass. Garnish rim with half an orange slice.

Clam Digger

Tabasco and horseradish generate some heat in this sassy and saucy selection that'll brighten any brunch.

6 ounces Clamato juice
¾ teaspoon lime juice
2 dashes of Tabasco
⅛ teaspoon fresh horseradish
Salt and white pepper to taste
Green margarita salt
Celery stalk with leaves (optional)
Lime slice (optional)

Pour first 5 ingredients over ice in shaker and shake vigorously 10–15 seconds. Wet rim of old-fashioned glass with more lime juice, then coat with margarita salt. Carefully pour mixture into glass. If desired, add celery stalk and garnish rim with lime slice.

Fuzzy Navel

The first rule of entertaining: The host should have fun. Make it easy for yourself with this simple yet sophisticated favorite.

3 ounces peach nectar
3 ounces orange juice
Mint sprig

Pour peach nectar over ice in highball glass. Stir in orange juice. Garnish with mint sprig.

Gin & Tonic

Ginger ale goes upscale for your most lavish cocktail parties. The secret? A dash of orange extract to add excitement.

½ cup tonic water
½ cup ginger ale
Dash of orange extract
Lime slice

Pour first 2 ingredients over ice in collins glass. Add orange extract and stir briefly. Garnish rim with lime slice.

Ginger Mint Julep

Take off for the races (or just get in the mood) with this blue-ribbon Kentucky Derby favorite that's sure to become a winning tradition.

½ ounce crème de menthe syrup
Cracked ice
4 ounces ginger ale
Mint sprig

Pour crème de menthe over cracked ice in collins glass. Add ginger ale and top with mint sprig. Serve immediately.

Godfather

Epicureans will enjoy this palate-pleasing combination. Its light, crisp taste pairs well with a wide range of hors d'oeuvres.

1 ounce almond syrup
6 ounces ginger ale

Pour ingredients over ice in old-fashioned glass.

Grasshopper

Chocolate milk isn't just for kids. With the sophisticated addition of crème de menthe, this grasshopper is a very adult offering, indeed. (And if you want cookies with it, we won't tell!)

1 ounce crème de menthe syrup
1 ounce chocolate syrup
4 ounces cold milk

Pour ingredients over ice in shaker and shake vigorously 5 seconds. Pour all contents into highball glass.

Grenadine Mocktail

Here, the unpretentious club soda is made party-worthy with the simple additions of sweet, sour, and a cherry on top.

4 ounces cold club soda
½ ounce grenadine
½ ounce lime juice
Crushed ice
Maraschino cherry

Pour first 3 ingredients over crushed ice in highball glass. Stir briefly, then add maraschino cherry.

Grog

With the flavor of all that's fresh at the farmers' market, just-picked ripe fruit makes this a perfect pairing for a cheese tray. It's entertaining made easy.

¼ cup seedless red grapes
½ cup Concord grape juice
¼ cup cantaloupe chunks
¼ cup honeydew chunks
¼ cup cranberry juice
Sugar

Blend first 5 ingredients in blender at high speed until thoroughly blended. Wet rim of margarita glass, then coat with sugar. Carefully pour mixture into glass.

Harlem Cocktail

You don't have to wait for a snazzy soiree to stir up this jazzy juice. The sweet blend of fruit flavors makes it a great accompaniment to a pretty hors d'oeuvre tray.

3 ounces pineapple juice
½ ounce grenadine
Maraschino cherry
Pineapple slice

Pour first 2 ingredients over ice in shaker and shake until cold. Strain into cocktail glass. Spear maraschino cherry and pineapple slice with toothpick and add to drink.

Harvey Wallbanger

Discover the delights of this fruity little favorite. With the sweet addition of banana extract, it's a tasty take on the time-honored classic.

4 ounces fresh orange juice
Cracked ice
½ teaspoon banana extract
Orange slice

Pour orange juice over cracked ice in highball glass. Pour banana extract on top and stir briefly. Garnish rim with orange slice.

Hot Buttered Rum

*Perfect for fireside chats, this cold-weather combi-
nation of cinnamon, spice, and all things nice
will warm your heart and soul.*

8 ounces pineapple juice
1 ounce fresh lemon juice
10 whole cloves
2 cinnamon sticks
1 teaspoon rum extract
2 tablespoons sweet butter, softened

Combine first 4 ingredients in saucepan over
medium-high heat until boiling. Stir well and strain
into clear Irish coffee glass. Stir in rum extract then
butter. Serve immediately.

Kir Royale

*Open your home to guests with this festive varia-
tion on the Kir Royale. Served with hot canapés
and snacks, it's a real winner.*

2 ounces apple juice
6 ounces red grape juice

Pour ingredients over ice in highball glass and stir.

Mai Tai

Get your sweet rewards with an inventive fusing of almond, pineapple, and more. Unapologetically sensuous, this mai tai is a real pleasure.

5 ounces pineapple juice
½ ounce almond syrup
3 ounces cranberry juice
½ ounce lime juice
Pineapple slice (optional)

Pour first 4 ingredients into collins glass and stir. Add ice and garnish rim with pineapple slice, if desired.

Mango Margarita

Morning, noon, or night, this healthy concoction pairs as well with muffins as it does with appetizers.

¼ large mango, sliced
½ tablespoon honey
¾ cup ice-cold milk
¾ tablespoon cold plain yogurt
Green sugar crystals
Lime slice

Blend first 4 ingredients in blender at high speed 30 seconds. Wet rim of margarita glass, then coat with green sugar crystals. Carefully pour mixture into glass. Garnish rim with lime slice.

Manhattan

In search of the perfect offering for your most treasured guests? The melding of sweet and tart flavors makes this mocktail a number one choice for just about any occasion.

¾ cup apple cider
1 teaspoon grenadine
¼ teaspoon Angostura bitters
Maraschino cherry

Pour first 3 ingredients over ice in shaker and shake vigorously 10–15 seconds. Pour all contents into old-fashioned glass. Garnish with maraschino cherry.

Martini

Serve the best with this smooth mocktini. It's always in good taste.

Tonic water
Lemon-lime seltzer
Lemon twist

Half-fill martini glass with tonic water, then top off with lemon-lime seltzer. Add lemon twist.

Melon Ball

Cantaloupe chunks provide a rich addition to this blender drink. For your next summer soiree, offer this cold combo along with your warmest hospitality.

2 ounces orange juice
¼ cup cantaloupe chunks
¼ cup crushed ice

Blend ingredients in blender at high speed until smooth. Pour into cocktail glass.

Mimosa

Sunday brunch is a snap to serve with bakery croissants, your favorite egg dish, and party-perfect mimosas.

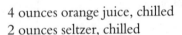

4 ounces orange juice, chilled
2 ounces seltzer, chilled

Pour ingredients into champagne flute.

Orange Colada

Influenced by the Caribbean classic, this mocktail is an ideal accompaniment to seafood dinners.

6 ounces fresh orange juice
1 teaspoon orange extract
⅛ teaspoon coconut extract
Cracked ice
Orange slice

Pour first 4 ingredients into shaker and shake well 10–15 seconds. Pour all contents into old-fashioned glass. Garnish rim with orange slice.

Piña Colada

Whip up some fun when you treat yourself and your friends to this outrageous offering.

3 ounces unsweetened pineapple juice
¾ teaspoon rum extract
1 ounce pineapple chunks
2 ounces Coco Lopez Piña Colada mix
1 ounce heavy cream
2 tablespoons shredded coconut
Maraschino cherry
Pineapple slice

Purée first 6 ingredients in blender at medium speed until thoroughly blended. Pour over ice in collins glass. Add maraschino cherry and garnish rim with pineapple slice.

Planter's Punch

Kick off your next party with a batch of this. Put on some island music, offer a tray of coconut shrimp, and grab a limbo stick.

6 ounces orange juice
1 ounce grenadine
1 ounce lime juice
4 ounces pineapple juice
Maraschino cherry

Pour first 4 ingredients over ice in collins glass and stir. Top with maraschino cherry.

Remsen Cooler

Back yard patio guests can cool off with this summer favorite. It's a wonderful accompaniment to barbecue and picnic suppers, too.

2 ounces cold lemonade
4 ounces cold tea

Pour ingredients over ice in old-fashioned glass and mix.

Rum & Cola

For idyllic evenings with your favorite friends, relax and unwind with this simple sipper and a tray of salty snacks.

8 ounces cold cola
¼ teaspoon rum extract

Pour ingredients over ice in old-fashioned glass. Stir briefly and serve immediately.

Screwdriver

Rediscover the pleasures of this beverage basic enhanced with orange extract. It's a zesty accompaniment to brunch or afternoon treats.

6 ounces fresh orange juice
1 teaspoon orange extract
Cracked ice
Orange

Pour first 3 ingredients into shaker and shake well 10–15 seconds. Pour all contents into old-fashioned glass. Garnish rim with orange slice.

Sea Breeze

Set your sights on serenity. Escape to your favorite easy chair with this cool, refreshing beverage that redefines fruit juice.

4 ounces grapefruit juice
4 ounces cranberry juice
Cracked ice

Pour ingredients into shaker and shake vigorously 15 seconds. Pour all contents into highball glass.

Sex on the Beach

Peachy? You bet. And when you pair it with a tray of crisp vegetable nibbles, you've got it made in the shade for a long, hot summer afternoon.

1 ounce peach nectar
3 ounces cranberry juice
3 ounces pineapple juice

Pour ingredients over ice in old-fashioned glass and stir.

Shirley Temple

Recall the joys of your childhood with this grown-up version of an innocent classic.

½ teaspoon grenadine
⅓ cup cran–raspberry juice
⅓ cup ginger ale
⅓ cup seltzer
Maraschino cherry

Pour first 2 ingredients over ice in collins glass and stir. Add ginger ale and seltzer. Garnish with maraschino cherry.

Siberian Sleigh Ride

Chill out with this delicious cream-and-coffee combo that is an ideal capper to any festive dinner menu.

1 ounce freshly brewed espresso, chilled
1 ounce heavy cream
Cracked ice

Pour ingredients into shaker and shake well 10 seconds. Pour all contents into brandy snifter.

Sidecar

Tart, tangy, and always appropriate. Here, the classic sidecar is updated with a refreshing twist. Offer it with a bowl of salted nuts, and you've got a party.

2 ounces red grapefruit juice
3 ounces orange juice
1 ounce lemon juice

Pour ingredients over ice in old-fashioned glass and stir.

Singapore Sling

The signature drink of any tropical vacation, our variation is just as tasty—without the alcohol. Try it and see.

1 ounce grenadine
½ ounce lime juice
4 ounces ginger ale

Pour ingredients over ice in old-fashioned glass.

Sloe Gin Fizz

When life gives you lemons, make up a serving of lemony Sloe Gin Fizz. Seltzer adds the bubbles. You might add a bowl of chips.

2 ounces lemonade
4 ounces seltzer
Lemon slice

Pour first 2 ingredients over ice in old-fashioned glass. Top with lemon slice.

Stinger

Life in the fast lane slows down with this mint-infused drink. Grab a glass of this refreshing sipper, then enjoy the scenery.

1 ounce crème de menthe syrup
5 ounces seltzer

Pour crème de menthe syrup over ice in old-fashioned glass, then top with seltzer. Stir briefly.

Strawberry Colada

Introduce your dinner guests to the joys of a superb strawberry colada. The essence of coconut is inspired by the tropics. Maybe you'll be inspired to dance the limbo.

4 ounces strawberry juice
1 ounce cream of coconut
Green sugar crystals
Strawberry slice

Pour first 2 ingredients over ice in shaker and shake well 10–15 seconds. Wet rim of margarita glass, then coat with green sugar crystals. Carefully strain mixture into glass. Garnish rim with strawberry slice.

Strawberry Daiquiri

Your favorite blender drink with an attitude. With zesty lime juice added for zip, you've gotta give this a whirl.

1 heaping cup fresh strawberries, washed
    with stems removed
1 tablespoon lime juice
2 tablespoons sugar
2 ounces cold water
4 ice cubes

Blend ingredients in blender at high speed 45 seconds. Pour into daiquiri glass.

Tequila Sunrise

*Morning glory! Treat your breakfast guests to a
tantalizing Tequila Sunrise. It's an amazing
accompaniment to eggs, toast, and the Sunday
newspaper.*

5 ounces soda water
1 ounce Torani Mandarin Orange Syrup
½ ounce Torani Grenadine Syrup
Orange slice
Maraschino cherry

Pour first 2 ingredients over ice in collins glass. Stir
well. Float Torani Grenadine Syrup on top by pouring
it slowly over an inverted teaspoon (rounded side up).
Garnish with orange slice and maraschino cherry.

Tropical Margarita

*Can't escape to a balmy island? Why not try
this magical mix of citrus favorites for a taste of
the tropics?*

¼ cup orange or grapefruit juice
3 tablespoons fresh pineapple juice
Crushed ice
¾ cup seltzer
Orange or grapefruit slice

Pour juices over crushed ice in shaker and shake vigorously 20 seconds. Pour all contents into margarita
glass. Add seltzer and stir briefly. Garnish rim with
orange or grapefruit slice.

Vodka Sour

Lazy afternoons on the porch call for this refreshing version of the classic. Quite nice when paired with chips and dips.

¾ ounce fresh lemon juice
1 teaspoon sugar
2 ounces water
Lemon twist
Maraschino cherry

Pour first 3 ingredients over ice in shaker and shake vigorously 15–20 seconds. Strain into cocktail glass. Garnish with lemon twist and maraschino cherry.

Whiskey Sour

All work and no play? Reward yourself with a tangy drink that goes great with your favorite sandwich.

Lime wedge
Sugar
Cracked ice
6 ounces grapefruit juice

Rub rim of old-fashioned glass with lime wedge, then coat with sugar. Add cracked ice and carefully pour grapefruit juice into glass. Garnish rim with lime wedge.

White Russian

Let the good times roll with our version of this rich, smooth classic. It'll bring a warm smile to your face.

4 ounces cold milk
2 ounces Coco Lopez Piña Colada mix
2 tablespoons chocolate syrup
Crushed ice
Ground cinnamon

Pour first 3 ingredients over ice in shaker and shake 10–15 seconds. Strain over crushed ice in old-fashioned glass. Dust ground cinnamon on top.

Woo Woo

Crisp cranberry juice matches perfectly with sweet peach nectar to produce this sublime sipper. Great for bridge night.

5 ounces cranberry juice
2 ounces peach nectar
1 teaspoon lime juice

Pour ingredients over ice in collins glass and stir.

Zombie

Here's an entertaining idea: Stir up some Zombies for your next get-together. The cool and refreshing blend of fruit flavors makes for a simple but impressive party drink.

4 ounces orange juice
4 ounces pineapple juice
1 ounce lime juice
½ ounce grenadine
Maraschino cherry
Orange slice
Lime slice

Pour first 4 ingredients over ice in collins glass and stir. Spear last 3 ingredients with toothpick and add to drink.

Drinks for All Seasons

Over a hundred creative drink recipes for holiday parties, special occasions, or any day of the year

Hot Cocoa l'Orange

*Does this drink sound divine, or what? With
the fusion of hot milk, cocoa, and orange zest,
it's perfect for a postdinner chat or nightcap.*

Topping

1½ tablespoons heavy cream, chilled
¼ teaspoon dark brown sugar (not packed)

Drink

1 large orange
1 cup milk
2 ounces premium milk chocolate, chopped
½ tablespoon unsweetened cocoa powder

Whisk together topping ingredients in bowl until
stiff peaks form. Cover and chill. Use vegetable
peeler to remove rind from orange. Place rind in
large saucepan. Add milk and bring to a simmer
over medium–high heat. Remove from heat and
cover. Allow to steep 20–30 minutes. Strain, then
return liquid to saucepan. Bring to simmer again
over medium–high heat. Whisk in chocolate and
cocoa powder until thoroughly melted and well
blended. Pour into Irish coffee glass and add
chilled topping.

Steaming Grapefruit & Spice

Get cozy with this spicy grapefruit treat that tastes great and is full of natural goodness, too. Offer a cup to your guests and get ready for rave reviews.

½ tablespoon superfine sugar
¼ cinnamon stick
¼ teaspoon whole cloves
12 ounces fresh grapefruit juice

In small saucepan stir ingredients together constantly over medium heat until hot. Strain into coffee mug or Irish coffee glass.

Cardamom Coffee

Wake up on a chilly day with coffee that gets its zing from a secret ingredient: cardamom. Served over ice, it really rocks.

½ teaspoon cardamom seeds
12 ounces cool water
4 tablespoons ground coffee
1 cup cracked ice
Sugar to taste
Pineapple slice (optional)

Boil cardamom seeds in water several minutes. Strain into coffeemaker, then brew coffee. Pour over cracked ice in collins glass and add sugar. Garnish with pineapple slice if desired.

Pineapple-Buttermilk Glacier

*What makes this so inviting? Cold buttermilk
that adds a rich texture and complex taste. Offer
it with a plate of muffins for an anytime treat.*

1⅜ ounces chopped pineapple
¾ cup cold buttermilk
1 tablespoon honey
¼ teaspoon vanilla extract
¼ cup crushed ice

Blend ingredients in blender at high speed until
smooth. Pour into margarita glass.

Tropical Fruits & Nuts Smoothie

*Granola on the run! This smoothie is the perfect
blend for a back-to-nature breakfast.*

1 cup ice-cold spring water
1 large banana, sliced then frozen
3 ounces sunflower seeds
3 ounces golden raisins

Blend ingredients in blender at medium speed 1
minute. Pour into frosted hurricane glass.

Rich & Creamy Hot Chocolate with Fresh Raspberries

Heart-warming (and tummy-warming) hot chocolate is made all the more enticing with the addition of a raspberry garnish. It's elegant enough for your posh gatherings.

½ cup heavy cream
¼ cup whole milk
½ tablespoon sugar
Pinch of salt
1½ ounces premium bittersweet chocolate chips
1 teaspoon sweet butter
Whipped cream (optional)
Fresh raspberries

In small saucepan bring first 4 ingredients to a boil over medium heat, whisking constantly. Stir in chocolate chips and butter and reduce heat to low. Continue stirring until chocolate is completely melted and mixture is smooth. Pour into Irish coffee glass. If desired, top with whipped cream. Sprinkle raspberries on top.

Festive Banana Buttermilk with Honey

Yum's the word. Settle down before a roaring fire and sip on this. You won't be disappointed.

1 small banana, sliced
½ cup cold, fresh buttermilk
½ teaspoon honey
Ground cinnamon (optional)

Blend first 3 ingredients in blender at high speed until smooth and creamy. Pour into white wineglass and dust ground cinnamon on top if desired.

Iced Orange Pekoe Tea with Cinnamon & Cloves

Quick and easy, but oh-so satisfying. Goes great with pumpkin bread or homemade cookies.

1 orange pekoe tea bag
Dash of ground cinnamon
Dash of ground cloves

Prepare tea according to directions, then steep with spices 10 minutes. Chill before serving over ice in collins glass.

Sparkling Cranberry with Lime

*This snappy cranberry potion will sparkle for all
your winter parties. For a swell effect, offer it with
cheese and crackers before your holiday dinners.*

8 ounces cranberry juice
2 ounces club soda
Lime slice

Pour cranberry juice over ice in collins glass. Add
club soda and stir briefly. Garnish rim with lime slice.

Angostura Ale

*A sophisticated drink to accompany your best hors
d'oeuvres. Serve with exquisite cheeses and pâté
for an extra-elegant party.*

1 teaspoon Angostura bitters
5 ounces ginger ale
Lemon slice

Pour bitters over ice in collins glass. Add ginger ale,
garnish with lemon slice, and serve immediately.

Hot Apple Buttered Rumless

*When the occasion calls for something special,
this piping hot buttered cider will do the trick.
Subtly spiced, it looks, smells, and tastes just
marvelous.*

Butter Mixture

¾ cup brown sugar, packed
½ cup margarine or butter, softened
¼ teaspoon finely shredded lemon peel
¼ teaspoon ground cinnamon
¼ teaspoon ground allspice

5 cups Martinelli's Cider or Apple Juice
10 teaspoons rum extract

For butter mixture, mix ingredients in small mixing
bowl until well combined.★ For each serving, place
1 rounded tablespoon of butter mixture in coffee
mug. Bring Martinelli's Cider or Apple Juice to a
boil, then pour into mugs. Add 1 teaspoon rum
extract to each. Stir well.

Yield: 10 servings

★ Use immediately or cover and chill up to 1 month.

Apple Cider à la Mode

Here, apple cider gets all dressed up. It's a fine accompaniment to any casual brunch.

8 ounces Martinelli's Sparkling Cider
1 scoop vanilla ice cream
Cinnamon to taste
Whipped cream
Nutmeg
Apple wedge

Blend first 3 ingredients in blender at high speed until well blended. Pour into hurricane glass. Top with whipped cream and dust with nutmeg. Add apple wedge on rim.

White Christmas Hot Chocolate

*Waiting for Santa? Nothing helps soothe the
suspense like hot chocolate and the spirited
addition of crushed candy canes.*

12 ounces whole or low-fat milk
1¼ ounces premium white chocolate, finely
  chopped
1 ounce peppermint or spearmint candy canes,
  crushed
Pinch of salt
Whipped cream

Pour milk into saucepan and bring to a simmer over
medium heat. Reduce heat to medium-low. Add
chocolate, half of crushed candy canes, and salt.
Whisk until smooth and creamy, then pour into
clear coffee mug. Top with whipped cream and
sprinkle remaining crushed candy canes on top.

Sparkling Christmas Mocktail

*Capture the holiday spirit with this red and green
specialty that should stir up lots of fun at gatherings big or small.*

1 ounce grenadine
4 ounces seltzer
Green sugar crystals

Mix first 2 ingredients in mixing glass. Wet rim of
cocktail glass, then coat with green sugar crystals.
Carefully pour mixture into glass.

Quick Party Eggnog

Holidays are the perfect time to share peace, good-will, and hearty cups of eggnog with family and friends. Laced with nutmeg, it's sure to add spice to any festive gathering.

1 cup cold eggnog
⅓ tablespoon ground cinnamon
⅓ banana
⅔ tablespoon real maple syrup
⅓ tablespoon ground nutmeg

Blend ingredients in blender at medium speed 30 seconds. Pour into balloon glass and dust top with more nutmeg.

Cold Chocolate Peppermint

Jingle your bells with the delicious duo of chocolate and peppermint. It's a can't-miss combination for the holidays.

2 scoops premium chocolate ice cream
1 cup cold milk
Dash of peppermint extract
Chocolate shavings
Peppermint candy cane

Blend first 3 ingredients in blender at medium speed until smooth and creamy. Pour into collins glass. Sprinkle chocolate shavings on top and add candy cane.

Cranberry-Apple Wassail

When your guests come in from a holiday sleigh ride, they'll smell the aromas of cinnamon and spice. But just wait until they taste this brew!

8 cups cranberry juice
3 cups apple juice
5 small cinnamon sticks
⅓ cup sugar
¾ teaspoon ground nutmeg
1 teaspoon whole cloves
5 orange slices, seeded
3 lemon slices, seeded

In saucepan bring first 6 ingredients to a boil over medium-high heat. Reduce heat and cover. Simmer 10 minutes. Strain into heat-resistant punch bowl. Add fruit slices.

Yield: 13 9-ounce servings

Kosher Toaster

Add a holiday glow to your Festival of Lights with kosher grape juice that's fancied up to celebrate the season.

Kosher grape juice
Crushed ice
Lemon slice (optional)

Pour juice over crushed ice in old-fashioned glass. If desired, garnish rim with lemon slice.

Sparkling Shampagne

The simple pleasures of this dishy little offering prove that less is more. It's simply sensational.

White grape juice, chilled
Cold seltzer

Fill champagne flutes ⅓ full with white grape juice. Top off each with seltzer.

Pink Shampagne

Mark the dawn of another year with this fun bubbly. Cheers!

1 ounce cran-apple juice, chilled
1 ounce apple juice, chilled
2½ ounces cold ginger ale

Pour first 2 ingredients into mixing glass and stir well. Add ginger ale and stir briefly. Pour into champagne flute and serve immediately.

Cold Duck

Ring in the New Year with a toast to good times and good friends. Festive and fizzy, this sparkling cooler is a party in a glass.

White grape juice, chilled
Sparkling water, chilled

Half-fill white wineglasses with white grape juice. Top off each with sparkling water.

Appellation Concord Brut

*When it's time for a toast, raise a glass of this
healthy bubbly.*

Concord grape juice, chilled
Ice-cold seltzer

Half-fill champagne flutes with grape juice, then
top off each with seltzer. Serve immediately.

Torani Super Bowl Sundae Latte

*Score lots of points and major kudos at your
Super Bowl party with this awesome blend of
chocolate and other flavors. Your evening may
go into overtime.*

½ ounce Torani Chocolate Mocha Sauce
⅛ ounce Torani Caramel Syrup
⅛ ounce Torani Almond Syrup
6 ounces milk
3 ounces freshly brewed espresso
Foamed milk

Stir together first 4 ingredients in small saucepan.
Heat over medium heat until hot. Pour into Irish
coffee glass to within ½ inch of top. Add espresso.
Top with thin layer of foamed milk.

Apple Ale

Got Super Bowl fever? Tart apple juice plays off the sweetness of ginger ale in this beverage that's perfect for toasting your team.

6 ounces ginger ale
6 ounces apple juice

Combine ingredients in mixing glass, then pour into frosted beer mug.

Pink Passion Frappé

Set a seductive mood for a Valentine's Day dinner with this pink and passionate pairing of fruit juices. The whipped cream topping makes it perfect for dessert (unless you have other ideas).

2 ounces Martinelli's Sparkling Cider
2 ounces pineapple juice
2 ounces cranberry juice
Whipped cream
Lime slice
Maraschino cherry

Blend first 3 ingredients with ice in mixing glass. Strain into champagne flute. Top with whipped cream. Garnish with lime slice and maraschino cherry.

Acapulco Sunset

*In the mood for love on Valentine's Day? Create
an aura of romance and linger over this sensuous
sipper that goes great with chocolate.*

1 cup fresh strawberries, sliced
½ cup papaya, chopped and seeded
1 ounce lime juice
10 ounces Martinelli's Sparkling Cider
Crushed ice
2 whole strawberries

Blend first 4 ingredients in blender at high speed
until smooth and thoroughly mixed. Pour over
crushed ice in 2 collins glasses. Garnish each rim
with whole strawberry. Serve with straws.

Yield: 2 servings

Sparkling Strawberry Kiwi

*You and your valentine can start a spectacular
evening with this pretty pink sparkler. Decadent,
delicious, and quite delightful. (Both the drink
and you.)*

V8 Splash Strawberry Kiwi Juice, chilled
Cold seltzer

Half-fill champagne flutes with juice. Top off with
seltzer.

The Big Easy

*Mardi Gras, Party Gras. This fizzy fun in a
glass is de rigueur for any carnival party.*

2 ounces half-and-half
Crushed ice
5 ounces cola
Maraschino cherry (optional)

Pour half-and-half over crushed ice in collins glass.
Top with cola and stir briefly. Add maraschino
cherry if desired.

New Orleans Day

*When the saints go marching in, raise a glass full
of frivolity. Perfect for your Mardi Gras brunch,
this creamy concoction really packs a punch.*

2 ounces Coco Lopez Cream of Coconut
1 ounce butterscotch topping
1 ounce half-and-half
1 cup ice

Blend ingredients in blender at high speed until
smooth. Pour into old-fashioned glass.

Iced Papaya Tea

Here, exotic papaya combines with traditional tea to produce an amazing blend of fruit-flavored fun.

8 ounces freshly brewed tea, hot
½ cup fresh papaya slices
Crushed ice

Pour tea into serving pitcher and add papaya. Chill until cold. Pour over crushed ice in collins glass.

Banana-Strawberry Mockery

Think pink! Bananas and strawberries come together in a treat that's (almost) too beautiful to drink.

1 banana, sliced
¼ cup strawberries
½ cup cracked ice
½ cup half-and-half, chilled
Sugar
Strawberry slice

Blend first 4 ingredients in blender at high speed until thoroughly blended. Wet rim of margarita glass, then coat with sugar. Carefully pour mixture into glass. Garnish with strawberry slice.

Melon Menagerie

*Springtime at the farmers' market offers ripe
and ready melons for the picking. Put them all
together to tickle your taste buds.*

⅓ cup cantaloupe chunks, seeded and chilled
⅓ cup honeydew chunks, seeded and chilled
⅓ cup watermelon chunks, seeded and chilled
2 ounces pineapple juice, chilled
Pineapple slice or maraschino cherry

Blend first 4 ingredients in blender at high speed
until smooth. Pour into margarita glass and garnish
with pineapple slice or maraschino cherry.

Survivor's Island

*Be a bon vivant with this enticing island favorite
that is an elegant addition to any occasion—
tropical or not.*

1 ounce grenadine
1 medium banana, sliced
2 ounces orange juice
2 ounces half-and-half
Crushed ice

Blend ingredients in blender at high speed 20 seconds. Pour into old-fashioned glass.

Iced Cajun Coffee

Coffee fanatics, take note: Cold milk infused with chilled espresso makes for a great waker-upper when you're on the go. It's a snap to make.

4 ounces very strong espresso, chilled
8 ounces cold whole milk
1 teaspoon vanilla extract
Ground cinnamon or nutmeg (optional)

Pour first 3 ingredients into mixing glass and blend well. Pour over ice in collins glass. Dust top with cinnamon or nutmeg if desired.

Key West Sunset

When spring's in the air, you've gotta get outside. Enjoy it with the taste of orange juice in a drink that's a real delight.

2 ounces fresh orange juice
½ ounce grenadine
5 ounces ginger ale
Orange slice (optional)

Pour first 2 ingredients over ice in shaker and shake well 10–15 seconds. Strain over ice in collins glass. Add ginger ale and stir briefly. Garnish rim with orange slice if desired.

Nectarine Lemonade

Here's a great idea for your picnic Thermos. The mystery ingredient? Nectarine tempered with lemon. This lemonade can accompany just about any outdoor menu.

2 nectarines
3½ cups water
1 cup fresh lemon basil leaves
¾ cup sugar
1 cup fresh lemon juice

Wash nectarines in cool water and remove pits. Coarsely chop one and place in small saucepan with 2 cups water, basil leaves, and sugar. Bring to a boil over high heat, stirring constantly. When sugar is dissolved, remove from heat. Cover and allow to steep several minutes. Uncover and allow to cool. Strain into serving pitcher. Stir in remaining 1½ cups water and lemon juice. Pour over ice in old-fashioned glasses. Slice remaining nectarine into thin wedges and use to top drinks.

Yield: 4–6 servings

Tropical Breeze

This drink will put you in a tropical state of mind. When you taste the coconut cream, you'll want to do the hula.

1 ounce cream of coconut
1 medium banana, sliced
1 ounce half-and-half
½ cup crushed ice
Sugar

Blend first 4 ingredients in blender at high speed until smooth. Wet rim of margarita glass, then coat with sugar. Carefully pour mixture into glass.

Citrus Twister

When citrus meets seltzer, it's a feast for the senses. What a welcome addition to any spring-time meal.

3 ounces orange juice
3 ounces pink grapefruit juice
½ teaspoon lime juice
2 ounces seltzer
Lime twist

Pour juices over ice in shaker and shake well several seconds. Strain over ice in old-fashioned glass. Top with seltzer, stir briefly, and garnish with lime twist.

Orange Iceberg

For a change of pace, team sherbet with orange juice. It's a wonderful accompaniment to late-night conversations in pretty spring settings.

4 ounces fresh orange juice, chilled
4 ounces cold seltzer
1 scoop orange sherbet
Orange slice

Pour juice into collins glass, then add seltzer and stir briefly. Float orange sherbet scoop on top. Garnish rim with orange slice.

Tropical Island

Satisfy your sweet tooth with the invigorating flavors of orange and lime. Serve after dinner with any chocolate pastry or as a teatime treat.

6 ounces orange juice, chilled
1 scoop lime sherbet

Pour juice into parfait glass, then float lime sherbet scoop on top. Serve with straw and spoon.

Banana Hurricane

*When banana meets ice cream, it's a beautiful
thing. The seductive flavors will send you spinning.*

1 banana, sliced
1 scoop vanilla ice cream
1 tablespoon chocolate syrup
1 cup milk
Chocolate shavings

Blend first 4 ingredients in blender at high speed
20–30 seconds. Pour into hurricane glass and top
with chocolate shavings.

Tropical Dream

*Serve up this cool tropical delight with warm
hospitality at your next gathering.*

¼ cup strawberries, fresh or frozen
1 banana, sliced
½ cup cracked ice
2 ounces pineapple juice
Mint sprig

Blend first 4 ingredients in blender at high speed
15–20 seconds until thoroughly mixed. Pour into
margarita glass. Garnish with mint sprig.

Peach Sparkler

Peach juice and seltzer provide an artful pairing of flavors. Try it and see.

½ cup peach juice
Cracked ice
½ cup seltzer

Pour peach juice over cracked ice in balloon glass. Add seltzer and stir briefly.

Raspberry Down Under

The fusion of raspberry, kiwi fruit, and almond butter creates a tart and creamy taste that's like no other.

1 cup raspberry juice, chilled
2 kiwi fruit
1 tablespoon almond butter
1 banana, sliced
2 tablespoons plain yogurt

Blend ingredients in blender at high speed until thoroughly mixed. Pour into daiquiri glasses.

Yield: 2 servings

Sparkling Blueberry

The secret to this drink's success? It's all in the
seltzer water—it adds the sparkle and the pizzazz.

¼ cup fresh blueberries
¼ cup seedless red or white grapes
Pinch of ground ginger
½ cup seltzer

Purée first 3 ingredients in blender at medium speed
1 minute. Add seltzer and blend at low speed 5 seconds. Pour into champagne flute.

Moroccan Peppermint Tea

Offer up a toast to good times and good friends
when you enjoy this refreshing sipper at your
next get-together.

⅓ cup fresh peppermint leaves, loosely packed
Sugar to taste
1 tablespoon green tea or 1 tea bag
1 cup boiling water
Mint sprigs

Combine first 3 ingredients in saucepan and add
boiling water. Allow to steep 5–10 minutes. Strain
into teacup. Garnish with mint sprigs.

Fancy Tropical Banana Punch

Our prediction? You and your party guests will love this smooth and seductive blend that's totally delicious and easy to make.

3 cups mashed bananas
1 cup lemon juice
2 cups light cream
2 cups sugar
5 cups ginger ale
1 pint each of lime, pineapple, and orange sherbet

Blend first 4 ingredients in blender at high speed until thoroughly mixed. Pour into punch bowl. Add ginger ale and chill in refrigerator. Float scoops of lime, pineapple, and orange sherbet on top just before serving.

Yield: 10 8-ounce servings

Chocolate Chai Tea

Sweetened condensed milk and chocolate flavoring make this tea a necessary luxury. Whip up a glass after a long, hard day.

1 cup crushed ice
¼ cup spiced chai tea
¼ cup seltzer, chilled
⅛ cup sweetened condensed milk
½ teaspoon sweetened chocolate powder

Blend ingredients in blender at medium speed until smooth. Pour into cocktail glass and serve immediately.

Special St. Patrick's Punch

Leaping leprechauns! Lime-flavored gelatin, fruit juices, and sherbet add up to a sensational St. Patrick's Day refreshment. Since you'll make most of it ahead of time, you won't miss any of the festivities.

2 3-ounce packages lime-flavored gelatin
2 cups boiling water
1½ cups sugar
1 12-ounce can frozen orange juice concentrate
1 12-ounce can frozen lemonade concentrate
2 cups cold water
1 12-ounce can pineapple juice
1 quart ginger ale
1½ quarts lime sherbet

In large heat-resistant bowl dissolve gelatin in boiling water. Add sugar and stir well. Prepare orange juice and lemonade according to directions. Add to bowl with cold water and pineapple juice. Mix well. Refrigerate overnight. Before serving, add ginger ale and scoops of lime sherbet.

Yield: 40 6-ounce servings

Green Leprechaun's Brew

Brew up some St. Patrick's Day fun to take to the parade. A fresh kiwi fruit slice gives it a little o' the green, so you'll pass the leprechauns' test.

5 ounces cold Tropicana Twister White
  Grape Kiwi
5 ounces cold seltzer
Kiwi fruit slice

Pour first 2 ingredients over ice in collins glass and stir briefly. Garnish rim with kiwi fruit slice.

Torani Iced Classic Irish Cream

This is no blarney: Leprechauns in the know celebrate all their St. Patrick's Days with this traditional and tasty favorite.

½ ounce Torani Irish Cream Syrup
2 shots espresso, chilled
8 ounces cold milk
Whipped cream
Chocolate shavings

Pour first 3 ingredients over ice in Irish coffee glass. Stir well. Top with whipped cream and chocolate shavings.

Relaxing Oriental Ginger Tea

You can relax on April 15 with a flavorful and calming cup of ginger tea. It's easy to make—nothing taxing about it.

1½ cups water
1 ounce fresh ginger root, thinly sliced
½ tablespoon honey or light brown sugar
Lemon wedge

Pour water into small saucepan. Add ginger and simmer over medium-low heat 20 minutes (or longer for stronger tea). Add honey or brown sugar and stir well. Strain into coffee mug. Garnish with lemon wedge.

Banana-Chamomile Nightcap

April 15 is a day of many happy returns. Chill out with this drink and think about how you'll be better organized next year.

⅔ tablespoon freshly brewed chamomile tea, chilled
1 banana, sliced
⅔ cup rice milk
⅔ tablespoon real maple syrup
Cracked ice

Blend first 4 ingredients in blender at high speed 15 seconds until thoroughly mixed. Pour over cracked ice in cocktail glass.

Devil's Dew

It's tax day: shoeboxes full of receipts, advice from your CPA brother-in-law, and a splitting head-ache. What do you need? The Devil's Dew— it's a smart and sassy concoction that will clear your mind.

3 ounces pineapple juice
2 ounces tomato juice
½ teaspoon lime juice
Lime slice

Pour juices over ice in shaker and shake well 10–15 seconds. Strain into old-fashioned glass. Garnish rim with lime slice.

Lemon-Ginger Energizer

Celebrate Earth Day with an energizing tea drink you make from scratch. Prepared with gin-ger, honey, and lemon, it's a natural winner.

Sliver of fresh ginger root, peeled
1 ounce honey
Zest from ½ lemon
1 cup water
1 ounce lemon juice
Lemon wedge (optional)

In small saucepan bring first 5 ingredients to a boil. Remove from heat. Cover and allow to steep 45 minutes. After mixture cools, strain over ice in collins glass. Garnish with lemon wedge if desired.

Rainbow Seltzer

Celebrate Earth Day with an au naturel fruit juice taste. Besides being healthy, it's cool, crisp, and contemporary.

Fruit juices in various colors
Seltzer
Lime slice

Pour fruit juices into ice cube trays and freeze. Fill collins glass with juice ice cubes in each color. Top off with seltzer. Garnish rim with lime slice.

Iced Spiced Tea with Mint

Whether you're watching the Kentucky Derby from the VIP box or your own living room, put your money on this spiced tea. It's a winner.

½ tablespoon dried mint leaves
½ tablespoon honey
1 cup steeped chai tea, chilled
¼ cup rice milk

Blend ingredients in blender at medium speed 30 seconds. Pour over ice in collins glass.

Cider Julep

Want to win by more than a nose? Then offer this new take on a Kentucky Derby tradition. It'll be your blue-ribbon best.

1 cup Martinelli's Cider or Apple Juice
¼ cup pineapple juice
¼ cup orange juice
1 tablespoon lemon juice
Fresh mint leaves

Mix first 4 ingredients in mixing glass and pour over ice in collins glass. Top with mint leaves.

Ginger-Apple Cooler

The tantalizing taste of ginger adds an interesting twist to this amazing apple cooler. It's perfect for alfresco dining.

⅛ teaspoon powdered ginger
6 ounces apple juice, chilled
1 cup crushed ice

Blend ingredients in blender at high speed until smooth. Pour into highball glass.

Frozen Raspberry Heat Buster

Summer entertaining is a breeze with your blender and these simple ingredients. There's nothing simple about the taste, though.

6 ounces frozen raspberries
1 cup raspberry sherbet
1 cup cold milk
Lime slice

Blend first 3 ingredients in blender at high speed just until smooth and creamy. Pour into daiquiri glass. Garnish rim with lime slice.

Iced Turkish Coffee

*Enjoy your own magic carpet ride as you let this
iced Turkish coffee take you to the casbah.*

¼ cup fresh cold milk
¼ cup cold half-and-half
3 whole cardamom pods, crushed
Sugar to taste
4–6 ounces freshly brewed coffee, chilled

In small saucepan bring first 4 ingredients to a boil
over medium-high heat, stirring constantly. Immediately remove from heat. Allow to cool, then strain
into serving pitcher. Add coffee and stir well. Before
serving, pour over ice in collins glass.

Pineapple Sorbet Lopez

*Teamed with grilled fish or coconut shrimp, this
Caribbean favorite will keep 'em coming back
for more.*

1½ ounces Coco Lopez Cream of Coconut
2 ounces pineapple juice
1 scoop pineapple sherbet
1 cup cracked ice

Blend ingredients in blender at high speed until
smooth. Pour into old-fashioned glass.

Fresh Fruit Swirl

Summertime and the sippin' is easy. Serve up the best of the summer's fresh fruit and add finesse with lime sherbet.

¾ cup watermelon chunks, seeded
½ orange, sliced and seeded
¼ cup lime sherbet
⅛ lemon, seeded

Blend ingredients in blender at high speed until thoroughly mixed. Pour into old-fashioned glass.

Cherry Cola

Grenadine adds a fun variation to this classic. Want to go really retro? Team with corn chips and bean dip.

1 tablespoon grenadine
12 ounces cola, chilled
Maraschino cherry

Pour grenadine over ice in collins glass. Add cola and top with maraschino cherry.

Old-Fashioned Peaches & Cream

Everything's just peachy in this extravagant but easy-to-make concoction that's reminiscent of hand-churned ice cream at your family picnics. Offer with gingersnaps.

1 cup low-fat yogurt, plain or peach
1 cup peach slices, fresh or frozen
½ cup half-and-half

Blend ingredients in blender at high speed until thoroughly mixed. Chill in freezer 10 minutes before serving. Pour into old-fashioned glass.

Homemade Orange Soda

When you're feeling the heat, a homemade orange soda can cool you off quickly. Perfect for poolside picnics.

1 orange, seeded, sliced, and chilled
6 ounces orange sherbet
6 ounces sparkling mineral water, chilled

Blend first 2 ingredients in blender at high speed until thoroughly mixed. Pour into collins glass and slowly pour mineral water on top.

Cherry-Cheese Swirl

Inspired by to-die-for cherry cheesecake, here's a primo partner for your breakfast breads. Why not give it a whirl?

½ cup cottage cheese
1 cup frozen cherries
¼ cup milk

Blend ingredients in blender at high speed until smooth and creamy. Pour into parfait glass.

Orchard Mélange

Delightfully luxurious and luscious, you'll want to make this strawberry-citrus blend a specialty at your house.

¼ lemon, seeded
½ cup strawberries, fresh or frozen
¼ cup crushed ice
½ navel orange, seeded
⅛ grapefruit, seeded

Blend ingredients in blender at high speed until thoroughly mixed. Pour into highball glass.

Lemon Cola

Need a quick accompaniment to tidbits and munchies? This tart classic is just the ticket!

Juice from ¼ lemon
12 ounces cola, chilled
Lemon slice (optional)

Pour lemon juice over ice in collins glass. Add cola. Garnish rim with lemon slice if desired. Serve immediately.

Sparkling Pineapple Lemonade

The taste of pineapple is a nice accent to this thirst-quenching favorite. Team it with salted nuts, and you're set for a day in the hammock.

2 cups sugar
2 cups water
2 cups unsweetened pineapple juice
1 cup fresh lemon juice
2 cups seltzer
8 lemon slices (optional)

Combine sugar and water in saucepan. Bring to a boil over medium-high heat, stirring constantly. Once sugar is dissolved, simmer on low heat undisturbed 8–10 minutes. Remove from heat and cool. Stir in pineapple juice and lemon juice. Add seltzer. Pour over ice in collins glasses. Garnish each with lemon slice if desired.

Yield: 8 servings

Mango Magnificence

Introduce your guests to the mango. The beautifully colored, fleshy fruit is a marvelous match for your most intensely flavored appetizers.

1 large mango, sliced
Juice from ⅓ lime
⅓ cup crushed ice
1 cup seltzer

Blend first 3 ingredients in blender at high speed until thoroughly mixed. Add seltzer and blend 5 seconds. Pour into balloon glass.

Pineapple with Ginger Iced Tea

Add pineapple to iced tea for a sweet-and-tart twist. The ginger gives an extra kick.

1 cup freshly brewed orange pekoe tea,
   cooled
1 cup fresh pineapple chunks
½ cup crushed ice
¼ teaspoon powdered ginger
Sugar to taste

Blend first 4 ingredients in blender at high speed 15 seconds until well mixed. Pour over ice in collins glass. Stir in sugar.

Banana-Orange Frappé

Greet your guests with this icy invention at your next outdoor soiree. The fusion of pineapple and brown sugar makes it a great partner to grilled fish and chicken.

1 large banana, sliced and frozen
¾ ounce unsweetened pineapple juice
¾ tablespoon light brown sugar, packed
⅓ cup orange juice, chilled
⅔ cup crushed ice
1½ ounces light cream

Blend ingredients in blender at high speed until smooth. Pour into cocktail glass.

Healthy Tomato Juice Mocktail

If you think healthy means bland, get a load of this. With zingy Tabasco and Worcestershire sauces, it's good stuff.

1 cup tomato juice, chilled
Juice from ½ lemon
Dash of Worcestershire sauce
Tabasco to taste
Salt and pepper to taste
Cracked ice
Lemon wedge

Pour first 5 ingredients into mixing glass and stir well. Pour over cracked ice in old-fashioned glass. Garnish with lemon wedge.

Banana-Pecan Tropica

The nutty pairing of pecans and fruit juice makes this a surprising and scrumptious sipper for breakfast or lunch.

1 cup apple juice, chilled
½ banana, sliced
½ cup banana low-fat yogurt
¼ cup shelled pecans
¼ cup ice water

Blend ingredients in blender at high speed 15 seconds until well mixed. Pour into collins glass.

Pineapple-Carrot Mixer

Add fun to a bowl of pretzels with this hearty and healthy drink. It's a can't-miss combination.

½ teaspoon lemon juice
3 ounces carrot juice
3 ounces pineapple juice

Pour ingredients over ice in shaker and shake until very cold. Strain into cocktail glass.

Blushing Banana

Why not try this new take on the classic banana smoothie? It's as pretty as a picture and provides a pleasing contrast to your salty summer snacks.

½ cup cran-apple juice, chilled
½ cup fresh orange juice, chilled
½ banana, sliced

Blend ingredients in blender at high speed 15 seconds until smooth. Pour into margarita glass.

Citrus Orange Pekoe Tea

The quintessential summer drink, iced tea, is made all the more appealing with the addition of tangy grapefruit. Get a kick out of it!

½ cup freshly brewed orange pekoe tea,
    chilled
½ cup fresh grapefruit chunks, seeded

Blend ingredients in blender at medium speed 20–30 seconds. Pour over ice in collins glass.

Vanilla Cola

Who doesn't like vanilla? This aromatic flavoring adds oomph to any cola drink. Offer it with a big bowl of popcorn when neighbors drop in.

12 ounces ice-cold cola
1 teaspoon vanilla extract

Pour vanilla extract over ice in collins glass. Add cola and serve immediately.

Cranberry Twister

*I scream, you scream, we all scream for…cran-
grape juice. Here's an innovative pairing that's
wonderful with happy-hour snacking or all alone.*

8 ounces cran–grape juice
1 small scoop vanilla ice cream or frozen yogurt

Blend ingredients in blender at high speed until
smooth. Pour into red wineglass.

Carrot-Orange Frappé

*Carrot juice gets a healthy and tasty makeover
that brings the best to your breakfast table. Team
with a basket of freshly baked bran muffins.*

⅔ cup fresh orange juice, chilled
⅓ cup carrot juice, chilled
⅔ tablespoon lemon juice
⅔ cup crushed ice
Lime slice

Blend first 4 ingredients in blender at high speed
until smooth. Pour into collins glass. Garnish with
lime slice.

Strawberries & Cream

The delicious duo of strawberries and cream stands alone, here, as a dessert. You may even want to garnish it with mint leaves or chocolate shavings and offer it with prettily decorated cookies.

1 small scoop vanilla ice cream or yogurt
½ cup strawberries, fresh or frozen
½ cup cold milk

Blend ingredients in blender at high speed until thoroughly mixed. Pour into highball glass and serve immediately.

Cherry Soda Fountain

Remember when you hopped up onto the soda fountain stool and ordered this classic? This cherry soda is a refreshing trip down memory lane.

Crushed ice
1 ounce grenadine
4 ounces seltzer
½ teaspoon Rose's lime juice
Lime slice

Pour crushed ice into old-fashioned glass. Add next 3 ingredients and stir briefly. Garnish rim with lime slice.

Strawberry Frappé

*By the pool, at the park, or on the beach, a
frosty fruit smoothie goes great with appetizers
or stands well on its own. Put on the Beach
Boys and start jammin'!*

3 ounces strawberries, fresh or frozen
½ cup orange juice, chilled
1 tablespoon sugar
¼ cup lemon-lime soda
½ cup crushed ice
Lime wedge (optional)

Blend first 5 ingredients in blender at high speed
until smooth. Pour into margarita glass. Garnish
with lime wedge if desired.

Sparkling Chai Tea

*Chill out on a scorching summer day with
relaxing, refreshing chai tea. With sweetened
condensed milk, it's great for after-dinner chats.*

1 cup ice
¼ cup freshly brewed spiced chai tea, chilled
¼ cup seltzer, chilled
⅛ cup sweetened condensed milk

Blend ingredients in blender at medium speed
5 seconds. Pour into margarita glass and serve
immediately.

Refreshing Ginger-Mint Lemonade

Many people consider Memorial Day to be the first weekend of summer. What better way to kick it off than with a picnic complete with tart and refreshing lemonade?

1 ounce fresh mint leaves, chopped
1 tablespoon chopped fresh ginger
1 tablespoon honey
½ cup boiling water
1 tablespoon fresh lemon juice
Cold water
Lemon slice
Fresh mint sprig

Combine first 3 ingredients in heat-resistant bowl. Add boiling water and allow to steep 20–30 minutes. Strain into measuring cup. Add lemon juice and enough cold water to measure 1 cup total. Pour over ice in collins glass. Garnish with lemon slice and mint sprig.

Torani Zombie

Memorial Day means back yard barbecues and poolside parties. But with this offering, it won't be your everyday ho-hum get-together. You'll drink in the compliments.

½ ounce Torani Creme de Cacao Syrup
¼ ounce Torani Strawberry Syrup
¼ ounce Torani Vanilla Syrup
2 ounces pineapple juice
2 ounces orange juice
1 ounce lemon-lime soda
Strawberry slice

Pour first 6 ingredients over ice in collins glass. Stir and garnish with strawberry slice.

Stars & Stripes Mocktail

Nothing says Fourth of July like this patriotic trio of red, white, and blue. Serve it proudly— it's a blast!

Red-colored fruit punch
PowerAde Thirst Quencher Arctic Shatter (white)
PowerAde Thirst Quencher Mountain Blast (blue)
Seltzer

Pour each of first 3 ingredients into separate ice cube trays and freeze. Place ice cubes in cocktail glasses and pour seltzer into each.

Independence Day Lemonade

Hooray for red, white, and blue—and lemonade!
This lemon-berry freeze is such a blast, it'll set
off fireworks in your mouth.

6 lemons
4 cups water
1 cup sugar
½ cup blackberries, fresh or frozen
Lemon slices (optional)

Remove about 1 tablespoon of zest from lemons.
Squeeze enough juice from lemons to produce 1
cup. In small saucepan boil 2 cups water. Add sugar,
stirring until dissolved. Add zest and remove from
heat. Pour in remaining 2 cups water and allow to
cool. Purée blackberries in blender at low speed
until well mixed. Add lemon zest mixture and
lemon juice. Blend at low speed until mixed. Strain
into pitcher. Chill in refrigerator several hours.
Before serving, pour over ice in collins glasses.
Garnish each with lemon slice if desired.

Yield: 6 cups

Independence Day Mocktail

Strike up the band with some John Philip Sousa sounds and this summer-ready concoction. It's sure to become your Independence Day favorite.

Blue margarita salt
Frozen milk cubes
8 ounces vegetable juice
Dash of Worcestershire sauce
Celery stalk with leaves

Wet rim of balloon glass, then coat with blue margarita salt. Add frozen milk cubes. (To make, pour milk into ice cube tray and freeze.) Carefully pour vegetable juice over cubes, then add Worcestershire sauce and stir. Garnish with celery stalk.

Apple Sparkler

It's tailgating time and time to cheer on your team. Score big with this cold apple spritzer, then cheer some more.

⅓ cup ice-cold apple juice
Ice-cold seltzer

Pour apple juice into pilsner glass. Top off with seltzer. Serve immediately.

Red Sunset

Enjoy this tasty treat as you enjoy the last few days of warm weather. And while you're at it, why not stick a little umbrella on top?

6 ounces lemonade
½ ounce grenadine
Lemon slice

Pour lemonade over ice in cocktail glass. Top with grenadine. Garnish rim with lemon slice.

Veggie Mocktail

The addition of lime juice makes this drink tasty and tempting. What a delicious way to get your veggies!

8 ounces vegetable juice, chilled
1 teaspoon lime juice
Lime slice

Pour vegetable juice into collins glass, then add lime juice and stir. Garnish rim with lime slice.

Cranberry Collins

*Take an afternoon break with this cool collins
paired with a plate of cheese. It'll rev up your
engines.*

4 ounces cranberry juice
2 ounces lemonade
Ice
Club soda

Mix together first 2 ingredients in collins glass, then
add ice. Top off with club soda.

Tangy Orange Rind Tea

*Simple yet exquisite. The lively flavors of
orange peel and cloves make this one tea you'll
want to linger over.*

4 tablespoons dry orange rind
12 ounces water
1 whole clove (optional)

Bring water to a boil. Remove from heat, then add
orange rind. If desired, add whole clove. Allow to
steep 5–6 minutes. Pour into teacup.

Banana-Mango Mockery

*Mad about mangos? Bonkers over bananas?
Then this fruit-filled favorite is a super and
healthy choice.*

1 banana, sliced then frozen
½ cup pomegranate juice
1 mango, sliced, seeded, then frozen
2 cups ice-cold water

Purée all ingredients in blender at high speed until
fully blended. Pour into daiquiri glasses.

Yield: 2 servings

Iced Cardamom Café

*Spice is nice, and this coffee drink is ready in a
flash. What could be more fun?*

12 ounces freshly brewed coffee, chilled
⅛ teaspoon ground cardamom
Cracked ice

Mix coffee and cardamom in mixing glass. Pour
over cracked ice in collins glass.

Tamarind Cooler

*What makes this drink so good? It's the hint of
tamarind paste—the exotic oriental fruit flavor—
that enhances the tastes of ginger and brown sugar.
Serve with a plate of fortune cookies.*

¾ cup water
1 tablespoon light brown sugar, packed
½ tablespoon minced crystalized ginger
¼ tablespoon tamarind paste (sold at Thai and other
  Asian food markets)
¼ tablespoon fresh lemon juice
Lemon slice

In medium saucepan bring water to a boil, then
whisk in next 3 ingredients until thoroughly mixed.
Cool, then strain into pitcher. Stir in lemon juice.
Chill several hours. Pour over ice in collins glass.
Garnish with lemon slice.

Banana-Pecan Smoothie

*Savor the flavors of banana and nuts for breakfast,
for lunch, or for a midnight snack. Why not?*

1 banana, sliced
1 cup banana yogurt
1 cup apple juice
¼ cup shelled pecan halves

Purée ingredients in blender at high speed 30 seconds. Pour into balloon glass.

Refreshing Orange Pekoe Tea

The essence of fennel makes this fruity drink even more exotic. Goes great with an afternoon snack.

1 cup water
1 ounce honey
1 teaspoon fennel seeds
1 orange pekoe tea bag
1 3-inch lemon rind strip
2 tablespoons fresh lemon juice

In small saucepan bring first 3 ingredients to a boil, stirring constantly. Remove from heat and add tea bag and lemon peel. Allow to steep 5–6 minutes. Strain into heat-resistant bowl. Once cool, add lemon juice and chill covered 1–2 hours. Pour over ice in collins glass.

Sangria Touchdown Punch

It's halftime. Why don't you just salsa on over for a cup of this snappy Spanish sangria? You'll need the extra boost for the last two quarters.

6 ounces lemon juice
16 ounces orange juice
Sugar to taste
1 bottle (750 milliliters) nonalcoholic red wine
Orange, lemon, and lime slices

Mix together first 4 ingredients in pitcher until sugar is dissolved. Chill until ready to serve. Pour into punch bowl and garnish with fruit slices.

Frozen Grapefruit Mockery

There's no resisting the appeal of sweet grapefruit juice and tart cranberry. Put 'em together, but watch out. You could create a riot.

½ cup cold cranberry juice
½ cup pink grapefruit juice
4 tablespoons lemon sherbet
Lemon slice

Blend first 3 ingredients in blender at high speed until smooth. Pour into balloon glass. Garnish rim with lemon slice.

Coffee-Rum Soda

Have you tried this cool, creamy coffee? It just might become your all-time favorite.

1 cup strong coffee, freshly brewed and
   chilled
½ teaspoon rum extract
½ cup half-and-half
Sugar to taste (optional)
Seltzer

Mix together the first 4 ingredients in mixing glass. Pour over ice in collins glass. Top off with seltzer and stir briefly.

Chocolate New York Egg Cream

This classic chocolate egg cream will take you away to another time and another place. Sip and savor.

½ cup ice-cold milk
6 tablespoons chocolate syrup
1 tablespoon chocolate ice cream
1½ cups cold seltzer
Whipped cream
Chocolate shavings

In mixing glass blend first 3 ingredients thoroughly. Add seltzer and stir briefly. Pour into collins glass. Top with whipped cream and chocolate shavings. Serve with straw.

English Bitters

Kick off some good times for all your football crowds, whether they're there for the game or just the good cheer. This invigorating blend of bitter and sweet is a snap to make.

1 teaspoon Angostura bitters
5 ounces ginger ale
Lemon slice

Sprinkle bitters over ice in collins glass. Add ginger ale. Garnish with lemon slice.

Sparkling Apple-Grape Juice Punch

Need a pretty punch to accompany your next elegant dinner? Its terrific taste accents any meal perfectly.

1 cup peach or apricot nectar
1 orange, thinly sliced
½ cup sweetened sliced strawberries, frozen or
  fresh★
1 bottle (750 milliliters) Martinelli's Sparkling
  Apple-Grape Juice, chilled

Stir together first 3 ingredients in punch bowl or pitcher. Chill until ready to serve. Pour in Sparkling Apple-Grape Juice and stir to blend. Serve with ice block, ring, or cubes.

Yield: 10 8-ounce servings

★ If using fresh strawberries, first place slices in bowl
  and sprinkle with sugar to draw out juices.

Tropical Freeze Lopez

When it's time to get down island style, here's your drink. Serve with shrimp appetizers and turn on the reggae.

2 ounces Coco Lopez Cream of Coconut
1½ ounces orange juice
1½ ounces pineapple juice
1 cup ice

Blend ingredients in blender at high speed until smooth. Pour into highball glass.

Orange Sorbet Lopez

Get your just desserts with this icy cold fruit sorbet. Serve with a spoon, and try not to slurp.

2 ounces Coco Lopez Cream of Coconut
1 ounce orange juice
1 scoop orange sherbet
½ cup ice
Orange slice

Blend first 4 ingredients in blender at high speed until smooth. Pour into collins glass. Garnish rim with orange slice.

Harvest Moon

The air is crisp, the leaves are turning, and the moon is full. Celebrate autumn with a fizzy fruit cider, then sit back and enjoy.

2 ounces mango-orange juice
4 ounces Martinelli's Sparkling Cider
1 ounce orange juice
Red apple wedge

Blend first 3 ingredients with ice in mixing glass. Pour into tulip glass and garnish with red apple wedge.

Strawberry Lemonade Provincial

Celebrate Labor Day and mourn the end of summer with a glass of strawberry lemonade. With its berry-and-citrus zip, you won't even notice that the days are getting shorter.

3½ cups water
¾ cup sugar (or to taste)
2 3-inch lemon rind strips
½ teaspoon vanilla extract
2 cups sliced strawberries
1 cup fresh lemon juice
6 lemon rind strips (optional)

In saucepan bring first 4 ingredients to a boil over medium-high heat, stirring constantly. When sugar is dissolved, cover and lower heat to simmer 5 minutes. Add 1 cup strawberries, then bring to a boil over medium-high heat. Remove from heat and allow to cool. Strain into serving pitcher. Add lemon juice and stir well. Add remaining cup of strawberries. Pour over ice in collins glasses. If desired, garnish each with additional lemon rind strip.

Yield: 6 servings

Sparkling Rainbow Punch

Celebrate the fading days of summer at a Labor Day get-together with this quick and tasty punch.

2 10-ounce packages frozen raspberries without syrup, thawed
1 6-ounce can frozen pink lemonade concentrate, thawed
¼ cup sugar
1 1-liter bottle nonalcoholic champagne, chilled
1 2-liter bottle raspberry-flavored ginger ale or plain ginger ale, chilled

Blend first 3 ingredients in blender at high speed until smooth. Strain into large punch bowl. Add champagne. Chill 2 hours. Stir in ginger ale just before serving. Add ice ring. (Recipe below.)

Yield: 6 quarts

Ice Ring

Freeze 4½ cups water in 6-cup ring mold. Arrange some or all of following on top of ice: strawberries, raspberries, lemon slices, lime slices, kiwi fruit slices, orange slices, and kumquat slices. Let fruit extend above top of mold. Pour 1½ cups water over fruit, filling mold to within ½ inch of top; freeze. Before adding to punch, let ice ring stand at room temperature 5 minutes. Carefully remove from mold and place in punch bowl, fruit side up.

Halloween Punch

*Having a monster bash? Then what
you need is this primo punch. Its
imaginative blend of citrus sherbet
flavors is a perfect pairing with
Halloween treats, and it's no trick to make.*

1 12-ounce can frozen orange juice concentrate
1 12-ounce can frozen white grape juice concentrate
1 2-liter bottle lemon-lime soda, chilled
1 pint orange sherbet
½ pint lime sherbet

In a large punch bowl combine first 3 ingredients and
stir until blended. Float scoops of sherbets on top.

Yield: 20 8-ounce servings

Witches' Brew

*Whip up a batch of this Witches'
Brew and serve it in a pumpkin
shell. It's sure to thrill all your
favorite ghosts and goblins.*

½ gallon lime sherbet, softened
1 2-liter bottle ginger ale, chilled
Large cleaned-out pumpkin (optional)
Orange sherbet

Mix first 2 ingredients in large punch bowl until
well blended. If desired, pour punch into large
cleaned-out pumpkin. Using a melon baller, float
orange sherbet scoops on top.

Yield: 20 6-ounce servings

Orange Goblin

Werewolves and witches and ghosts, oh my! Give all the ghouls a sip of this colorful orange favorite. Sparkling seltzer makes it festive and fun.

4 ounces fresh orange juice, chilled
4 ounces seltzer, chilled
1 scoop orange sherbet
Orange slice

Pour orange juice into collins glass, then add seltzer. Float orange sherbet scoop on top. Garnish rim with orange slice.

Monster Mango

For a spooktacular and tasty trick-or-treat fest, go with ripe mango. It goes down smooth.

1 large mango, sliced, seeded, and chilled
Juice from ⅓ lime
⅓ cup crushed ice
1 cup seltzer
Lime slice

Blend first 3 ingredients in blender at high speed until thoroughly mixed. Add seltzer and blend briefly. Pour into balloon glass and garnish rim with lime slice.

Pumpkin à la Mode

It's Halloween! Gather up all your goblins for this tempting treat that's no trick to fix. It's simple, sweet, and super special.

1½ ounces canned pumpkin
⅛ teaspoon ground nutmeg
6 ounces ice-cold milk
3 ounces premium vanilla ice cream
⅛ teaspoon vanilla extract (optional)
⅛ teaspoon ground cinnamon
Ground cinnamon

Blend first 6 ingredients in blender at high speed 15–30 seconds or until thoroughly mixed. Pour into hurricane glass. Dust top with more ground cinnamon.

Orange Candied Yam

Make this drink a Thanksgiving tradition in your house—it's a sweet potato soufflé in a glass. We're surprised the Pilgrims didn't invent it!

2 tablespoons light brown sugar (not packed)
¼ banana
3 tablespoons small marshmallows
½ cup fresh orange juice
2 ounces cooked sweet potato

Blend ingredients in blender at high speed 30 seconds. Pour into cocktail glass.

Cranberry-Vanilla Party Punch

On this day of thanks, offer a special nod of gratitude to the tart, tangy cranberry. Then drink up!

18 ounces frozen strawberries
3 bananas, sliced
1½ cups vanilla ice cream
½ cup sugar
½ cup orange juice, chilled
6 cups cranberry juice, chilled

Blend first 5 ingredients and 1 cup cranberry juice in blender at high speed until smooth. Pour into large punch bowl. Add remaining cranberry juice and stir well.

Yield: 18 10-ounce servings

Cranberry & Walnut Smoothie

With a bounty of friends, food, and fun, Thanksgiving Day makes you feel so grateful. And this super smoothie is just one more thing to be thankful for.

½ cup vanilla yogurt
½ cup cranberry juice
⅛ cup shelled walnut halves

Blend ingredients in blender at high speed 15 seconds until smooth. Pour over ice in hurricane glass.

Sweet Endings

*Recipes for thirty scrumptious coffees,
teas, and ice-cream drinks*

Roasted French Chicory Coffee

Mmm.... Get a whiff of this full-bodied cuppa joe. With the melding of rich, dark chicory and soothing hot milk, it's a combination that can't be beat.

¾ scoop French roast ground coffee
½ scoop chicory ground coffee
12 ounces water
½ cup steamed milk, hot
Pinch of ground cinnamon

Brew coffees together. Pour into Irish coffee glass. Add steamed milk. Dust top with ground cinnamon.

Café au Lait

Ooo-la-la! This French classic is decadent, delicious, and oh-so delightful.

½ cup strong coffee, freshly brewed and hot
½ cup scalded light cream
Whipped cream
Cinnamon stick

Pour coffee into coffee mug. Add scalded cream. Top with whipped cream and add cinnamon stick.

Vanilla Bean Café

Wake up and smell the coffee, cinnamon, and vanilla bean. With flavors simmered just to their peak, it's aromatherapy for your soul.

¼ vanilla bean (sliced lengthwise) or ⅛ teaspoon
  vanilla extract
¼ cup milk
½ teaspoon light brown sugar, not packed
¼ teaspoon ground cinnamon
4 ounces freshly brewed coffee, hot

Place vanilla bean slices or extract in saucepan. Add milk and brown sugar, then bring to a boil, stirring constantly. Remove from heat and cover. Allow to steep 3–4 minutes. Remove bean slices and quickly whisk until frothy. Pour over coffee in Irish coffee glass.

Café l'Orange

Just for the fun of it, serve up a piping hot cup of café l'orange. Topped with fresh whipped cream and zesty orange peel, it's sinfully delicious.

1 cup rich French roast coffee or espresso, freshly
  brewed and hot
¼ cup fresh heavy cream, whipped
Grated orange peel

Pour coffee or espresso into coffee mug, then top with whipped cream. Sprinkle grated orange peel on top.

Vanilla Cream Extravaganza

Exceedingly simple yet extravagantly satisfying, the richness of egg white and fresh cream make this a perfect ending to a perfect meal.

1 large egg white or egg white substitute
½ cup fresh heavy cream
⅓ teaspoon vanilla extract
3 cups freshly brewed coffee, hot

Whisk egg white in small mixing bowl until stiff peaks form. In separate bowl whisk together cream and vanilla until light and airy. Mix egg white with cream mixture and pour into 4 clear coffee mugs. Pour coffee into each.

Yield: 4 servings

Arabic Coffee

Good taste makes for good times. This Arabic coffee, ready for sipping out of demitasse cups, is a flavor you'll want to savor.

1 tablespoon Arabic ground coffee (ground extremely fine)
1–2 teaspoons sugar
2 ounces cold water
Sliver of lemon rind (optional)

Combine first 3 ingredients in *ibrik* or small saucepan. Bring to a boil over high heat; do not stir. Remove from heat and carefully pour into demitasse cup. If desired, garnish with sliver of lemon rind.

Polynesian Island Coconut Coffee

Been snowed-in too long? Dreaming of an island vacation? Get the next best thing with this Polynesian coffee. Close your eyes, take a sip, and let the taste of coconut take you there.

½ cup milk
⅓ cup sweetened shredded coconut
½ cup freshly brewed coffee, hot

Preheat oven to 350°F. In small saucepan mix together first 2 ingredients over low heat 5 minutes. Allow to steep 1 minute, then strain. Spread shredded coconut on broiler pan and bake just until it browns (5–10 minutes). Pour coffee into mug and add strained milk. Top with toasted coconut.

Sweet Espresso Latte

Get your hands around a warm mug of this after-dinner pleaser. It's a delicious compliment to a delicious meal.

4 ounces freshly brewed espresso, hot
4 ounces warm milk
1 teaspoon honey

Stir ingredients together in coffee mug.

Chocolate-Lemon Espresso

Want a dishy accompaniment to your after-dinner biscotti? This lemon-chocolate warm-up is ideal for dipping, if you're so inclined.

1 cup whole milk
1½ ounces semisweet chocolate, finely chopped
½ tablespoon instant espresso powder
Sugar to taste
Lemon rind strip

In saucepan bring ingredients to a boil over medium-high heat, whisking constantly. Remove from heat. Allow to steep 1 minute, then strain into coffee mug.

Café Marnier

Take top honors with a special addition to your end-of-the-day treat. The subtle but sensational citrus flavoring makes this festive and fabulous.

½ teaspoon orange extract
8 ounces freshly brewed espresso, hot
Whipped cream

Pour orange extract into coffee mug, then stir in espresso. Top with whipped cream.

Cinnamon-Clove Tea

Experience the serenity of a spicy cup of tea and a quiet evening all to yourself. With steaming cinnamon and cloves, this is practically aromatherapy.

8 ounces boiling water
1 tea bag
Pinch of ground cinnamon
5 whole cloves
Sugar to taste

Steep together ingredients 5 minutes, then strain into teacup.

Ginger Tea

Long known to soothe upset tummies, this sweetened ginger tea will also soothe your soul.

½ ounce ginger root, thinly sliced
½ tablespoon honey or brown sugar
8 ounces boiling water
Lemon wedge

Steep together first 3 ingredients 5 minutes. Strain into coffee mug and garnish with lemon wedge.

Apple Tea with Honey

A taste of honey adds just the right amount of sweetness to any tea. It's what you've been waiting for.

8 ounces boiling water
1 tea bag
5 ounces apple juice, hot
2 teaspoons honey
½ apple slice

Pour water into coffee mug. Add tea bag and steep according to package directions. Remove tea bag. Stir in apple juice and honey. Place apple slice on top.

Spearmint Tea

Lighten up with the invigorating scent of fresh spearmint. It's positively uplifting!

⅓ cup spearmint leaves, loosely packed
Sugar to taste
1 tea bag
8 ounces boiling water

Steep together ingredients 5–10 minutes, then strain into teacup.

Orange Peel Tea

Cozy up with a good book and a cup of this brew. The melding of orange peel and cloves lends a distinctive and comforting flavor to the mix.

4 tablespoons dry orange rind
12 ounces boiling water
1 tea bag
2 whole cloves

Steep together ingredients 5–10 minutes, then strain into teacup.

Irish Tea

Crème de menthe is a subtle yet satisfying addition to an everyday mug of tea. It's enchanting.

8 ounces boiling water
1 tea bag
½ ounce crème de menthe syrup
Sugar to taste

Pour water into coffee mug. Add tea bag and steep according to package directions. Remove tea bag. Stir in last 2 ingredients.

Amaretto Green Tea with Honey

Amaretto flavoring and honey make this tea rich and smooth. It's always in good taste.

8 ounces boiling water
1 green tea bag
Amaretto flavoring (at least 3 drops)
Honey

Pour water into coffee mug. Add tea bag and steep according to package directions. Remove tea bag. Stir in last 2 ingredients.

Chamomile Nightcap

Your grandmother was right. Chamomile tea is an effective and delicious sleep aid. Sweet dreams!

8 ounces boiling water
1 chamomile tea bag
Honey
Cream (optional)

Pour water into coffee mug. Add tea bag and steep according to package directions. Remove tea bag. Stir in honey and cream if desired.

Apple-Cinnamon Tea

Got a craving for apples and cinnamon? Here's the solution, and it's simple to make, too. What are you waiting for?

6 ounces freshly brewed tea, hot
2 ounces apple juice, hot
Ground cinnamon

Combine first 2 ingredients in coffee mug. Dust top with cinnamon.

Oriental Almond Tea

The subtle taste of almond syrup makes this a perfect match for an Asian dinner or a fortune cookie snack.

8 ounces boiling water
1 Chinese breakfast tea bag
1 teaspoon almond syrup

Pour water into coffee mug. Add tea bag and steep according to package directions. Remove tea bag. Stir in almond syrup.

Mocha Ice-Cream Shake

Here's the scoop: Your favorite ice cream gets a coffee buzz. It's absolutely dreamy.

4 ounces espresso, chilled
1 ounce light cream
1 scoop premium vanilla ice cream, slightly softened
¼ cup seltzer

In mixing glass mix first 2 ingredients. Place ice cream in hurricane glass, then pour espresso mixture over top. Stir briefly. Slowly add seltzer and stir briefly.

Butterscotch Shake

With the smooth taste of butterscotch, this shake is sure to be a family favorite.

1 cup cold milk
1 scoop premium vanilla ice cream
2 tablespoons butterscotch syrup

Blend ingredients in blender at high speed until mixed. Pour into brandy snifter.

Nostalgic Creamsicle Float

*Re-create fond memories of your childhood with
this cool, creamy classic. Simple and satisfying.*

8 ounces fresh orange juice, chilled
1 scoop premium vanilla ice cream

Pour orange juice into hurricane glass. Float ice-
cream scoop on top.

Cocoa Café Float

*Chocolate is the "food of the gods." And when
chocolate meets coffee, it's a match made in
heaven.*

2 scoops premium chocolate ice cream
6 ounces freshly brewed coffee, chilled
¼ cup whipped cream
Powdered sweetened chocolate (optional)

Place ice cream in collins glass, then slowly pour
coffee over top. Top with whipped cream. If desired,
sprinkle powdered chocolate on top.

Banana-Almond Shake

Here's a frothy twist to the classic banana split.
There's just a hint of almond, so give it a whirl.

1 banana, sliced
2 scoops premium vanilla ice cream
1 cup cold milk
⅛ teaspoon almond extract
Whipped cream
Ground cinnamon

Blend first 4 ingredients in blender at high speed until smooth and creamy. Pour into collins glass. Top with whipped cream, then dust top with cinnamon.

Yield: 1–2 servings

Espresso Float Special

Get your kicks as cinnamon and espresso meld
into your favorite ice cream. It's the ultimate
indulgence.

4 ounces freshly brewed espresso, chilled
¼ cup milk
2 scoops premium vanilla ice cream
Whipped cream
Cinnamon stick

In mixing glass mix first 2 ingredients. Place ice cream in collins glass, then slowly pour espresso mixture over top. Top with whipped cream and garnish with cinnamon stick.

Chocolate-Strawberry-
Mocha Shake

Shake it up, baby! When you combine strawberries and chocolate with coffee and ice cream, you've got dessert in a glass.

2 scoops premium vanilla ice cream
2 cups cold milk
4 ounces espresso, chilled
1 cup strawberries, fresh or frozen
4 tablespoons premium chocolate syrup
Chocolate sprinkles

Blend first 5 ingredients in blender at high speed until smooth and creamy. Pour into hurricane glasses. Top each with chocolate sprinkles.

Yield: 4 servings

The Venerable Black Cow

Making this classic is a small-time effort for a big-time taste. No wonder it's survived the test of time.

2 scoops premium vanilla ice cream
8 ounces ice-cold cola

Place ice cream in hurricane glass, then slowly pour cola over top. Serve with spoon and long straw.

Old-Fashioned Root Beer Float

With a nod to malt shops of yore, revel in the nostalgic bliss of a good old all-American root beer float.

2 scoops premium vanilla ice cream
8 ounces ice-cold root beer

Place ice cream in hurricane glass, then slowly pour root beer over top. Serve with spoon and long straw.

Chocolate Black Cow

Splurge a little. You deserve to treat yourself every now and then. And this rich concoction is quite a treat.

2 scoops premium vanilla ice cream
1 tablespoon chocolate syrup
8 ounces ice-cold cola

Place ice cream in hurricane glass, then add chocolate syrup. Slowly pour cola over top.

Index

Acapulco Sunset, 44
Amaretto Green Tea with Honey, 104
Angostura Ale, 35
Appellation Concord Brut, 42
Apple Ale, 43
Apple cider. *See* Cider
Apple Cider á la Mode, 37
Apple-Cinnamon Tea, 105
Apple-Grape Juice Punch, 86
Apple juice
   Apple Ale, 43
   Apple-Cinnamon Tea, 105
   Apple Sparkler, 79
   Apple Tea with Honey, 102
   Banana-Pecan Smoothie, 82
   Banana-Pecan Tropica, 70
   Cider Julep, 61
   Cranberry-Apple Wassail, 40
   Ginger-Apple Cooler, 62
   Hot Apple Buttered Rumless, 36
   Kir Royale, 12
   Pink Shampagne, 41
Apple Cider á la Mode, 37
Apple Sparkler, 79
Apple Tea with Honey, 102
Arabic Coffee, 98

Banana-Almond Shake, 108
Banana Buttermilk with Honey, 34
Banana-Chamomile Nightcap, 58
Banana Hurricane, 52
Banana-Mango Mockery, 81
Banana-Orange Frappé, 69
Banana-Pecan Smoothie, 82
Banana-Pecan Tropica, 70
Banana-Strawberry Mockery, 46
Barware, v
Basic ingredients, viii
Big Easy, 45
Black Cow, 109
Black Russian, 2
Blarney Stone, 2
Blood & Sand, 3
Bloody Mary, 3
Blushing Banana, 71
Bocci Ball, 4
Brandy Alexander, 4
Butterscotch Shake, 106

Café au Lait, 96
Café l'Orange, 97
Café Marnier, 100
Cape Codder, 5
Cardamom Coffee, 31
Carrot-Orange Frappé, 72
Chamomile Nightcap, 104
Champagne, nonalcoholic
   Sparkling Rainbow Punch, 89
Cherry-Cheese Swirl, 66
Cherry Cola, 64
Cherry Gimlet, 5
Cherry Soda Fountain, 73
Chi Chi, 6
Chocolate
   Banana Hurricane, 52
   Black Russian, 2
   Brandy Alexander, 4
   Chocolate Black Cow, 110
   Chocolate Chai Tea, 55
   Chocolate-Lemon Espresso, 100
   Chocolate New York Egg Cream, 85
   Chocolate-Strawberry-Mocha
     Shake, 109
   Cocoa Café Float, 107
   Grasshopper, 9
   Hot Chocolate with Fresh
     Raspberries, 33
   Hot Cocoa l'Orange, 30
   Torani Super Bowl Sundae Latte,
     42
   White Christmas Hot Chocolate, 38
   White Russian, 26
Chocolate Black Cow, 110
Chocolate Chai Tea, 55
Chocolate-Lemon Espresso, 100
Chocolate New York Egg Cream, 85
Chocolate-Strawberry-Mocha
   Shake, 109
Christmas drinks
   Cold Chocolate Peppermint, 39
   Cranberry-Apple Wassail, 40
   Quick Party Eggnog, 39
   Sparkling Christmas Mocktail, 38
   White Christmas Hot Chocolate, 38
Cider
   Acapulco Sunset, 44
   Apple Cider á la Mode, 37

   Cider Julep, 61
   Harvest Moon, 87
   Hot Apple Buttered Rumless, 36
   Manhattan, 14
   Pink Passion Frappé, 43
Cider Julep, 61
Cinnamon-Clove Tea, 101
Citrus Collins, 6
Citrus Orange Pekoe Tea, 71
Citrus Twister, 50
Clam Digger, 7
Cocoa Café Float, 107
Coconut, cream of
   Chi Chi, 6
   New Orleans Day, 45
   Orange Sorbet Lopez, 87
   Pineapple Sorbet Lopez, 63
   Strawberry Colada, 23
   Tropical Breeze, 50
   Tropical Freeze Lopez, 86
Coffee drinks
   Arabic Coffee, 98
   Café au Lait, 96
   Café l'Orange, 97
   Café Marnier, 100
   Cardamom Coffee, 31
   Chocolate-Lemon Espresso, 100
   Chocolate-Strawberry-Mocha
     Shake, 109
   Cocoa Café Float, 107
   Coffee-Rum Soda, 84
   cold, 20, 31, 48, 57, 63, 81, 84,
     108, 109
   Espresso Float Special, 108
   Iced Cajun Coffee, 48
   Iced Cardamom Café, 81
   Iced Turkish Coffee, 63
   Mocha Ice-Cream Shake, 106
   Polynesian Island Coconut Coffee,
     99
   Roasted French Chicory Coffee, 96
   Siberian Sleigh Ride, 20
   Sweet Espresso Latte, 99
   Torani Iced Classic Irish Cream, 57
   Torani Super Bowl Sundae Latte,
     42
   Vanilla Bean Café, 97
   Vanilla Cream Extravaganza, 98

Coffee-Rum Soda, 84
Cola
    Big Easy, 45
    Black Cow, 109
    Cherry Cola, 64
    Chocolate Black Cow, 110
    Lemon Cola, 67
    Rum & Cola, 18
    Vanilla Cola, 71
Cold Chocolate Peppermint, 39
Cold Duck, 41
Cranberry & Walnut Smoothie, 93
Cranberry-Apple Wassail, 40
Cranberry Collins, 80
Cranberry juice
    Cape Codder, 5
    Cranberry & Walnut Smoothie, 93
    Cranberry-Apple Wassail, 40
    Cranberry Collins, 80
    Cranberry-Vanilla Party Punch, 93
    Frozen Grapefruit Mockery, 84
    Grog, 10
    Mai Tai, 13
    Pink Passion Frappé, 43
    Sea Breeze, 19
    Sex on the Beach, 19
    Sparkling Cranberry with Lime, 35
    Woo Woo, 26
Cranberry Twister, 72
Cranberry-Vanilla Party Punch, 93
Cream
    Banana-Orange Frappé, 69
    Cafe au Lait, 96
    Fancy Tropical Banana Punch, 55
    Hot Chocolate with Fresh
        Raspberries, 33
    Hot Cocoa l'Orange, 30
    Mocha Ice-Cream Shake, 106
    Piña Colada, 16
    Siberian Sleigh Ride, 20
    Vanilla Cream Extravaganza, 98
Creamsicle Float, 107
Créme de menthe
    Ginger Mint Julep, 8
    Grasshopper, 9
    Irish Tea, 103
    Stinger, 22

Devil's Dew, 59

Earth Day drinks
    Lemon-Ginger Energizer, 59
    Rainbow Seltzer, 60
Eggnog, 39
English Bitters, 85
Espresso Float Special, 108

Fancy Tropical Banana Punch, 55
Festive Banana Buttermilk with
    Honey, 34
Floats
    Black Cow, 109
    Chocolate Black Cow, 110
    Cocoa Café Float, 107
    Espresso Float Special, 108
    Nostalgic Creamsicle Float, 107
    Old-Fashioned Root Beer Float,
        110
Fourth of July drinks
    Independence Day Lemonade, 77
    Independence Day Mocktail, 78
    Stars & Stripes Mocktail, 76
Fresh Fruit Swirl, 64
Frozen Grapefruit Mockery, 84
Frozen Raspberry Heat Buster, 62
Fuzzy Navel, 7

Garnishes, viii–ix
Gin & Tonic, 8
Ginger ale
    Angostura Ale, 35
    Apple Ale, 43
    English Bitters, 85
    Fancy Tropical Banana Punch, 55
    Gin & Tonic, 8
    Ginger Mint Julep, 8
    Godfather, 9
    Key West Sunset, 48
    Pink Shampagne, 41
    Shirley Temple, 20
    Singapore Sling, 21
    Sparkling Rainbow Punch, 89
    Special St. Patrick's Punch, 56
    Witches' Brew, 90
Ginger-Apple Cooler, 62
Ginger Mint Julep, 8
Ginger Tea, 101
Glassware, vi–vii
Godfather, 9

Grapefruit juice
    Citrus Collins, 6
    Citrus Twister, 50
    Frozen Grapefruit Mockery, 84
    Sea Breeze, 19
    Sidecar, 21
    Steaming Grapefruit & Spice, 31
    Tropical Margarita, 24
    Whiskey Sour, 25
Grape juice
    Appellation Concord Brut, 42
    Cold Duck, 41
    Grog, 10
    Halloween Punch, 90
    Kir Royale, 12
    Kosher Toaster, 40
    Sparkling Shampagne, 41
Grasshopper, 9
Green Leprechaun's Brew, 57
Grenadine Mocktail, 10
Grog, 10

Half-and-half
    Banana-Strawberry Mockery, 46
    Big Easy, 45
    Black Russian, 2
    Brandy Alexander, 4
    Coffee-Rum Soda, 84
    Iced Turkish Coffee, 63
    New Orleans Day, 45
    Old-Fashioned Peaches & Cream,
        65
    Survivor's Island, 47
    Tropical Breeze, 50
Halloween drinks
    Halloween Punch, 90
    Monster Mango, 91
    Orange Goblin, 91
    Pumpkin á la Mode, 92
    Witches' Brew, 90
Halloween Punch, 90
Hanukah drink
    Kosher Toaster, 40
Harlem Cocktail, 11
Harvest Moon, 87
Harvey Wallbanger, 11
Healthy Tomato Juice Mocktail, 69
Homemade Orange Soda, 65
Hot Apple Buttered Rumless, 36
Hot Buttered Rum, 12

Hot chocolate
    White Christmas, 38
    with Fresh Raspberries, 33
Hot Cocoa l'Orange, 30

Ice, x
Ice cream
    Apple Cider á la Mode, 37
    Banana-Almond Shake, 108
    Banana Hurricane, 52
    Black Cow, 109
    Butterscotch Shake, 106
    Chocolate Black Cow, 110
    Chocolate New York Egg Cream, 85
    Chocolate-Strawberry-Mocha
        Shake, 109
    Cocoa Café Float, 107
    Cold Chocolate Peppermint, 39
    Cranberry-Vanilla Party Punch, 93
    Cranberry Twister, 72
    Espresso Float Special, 108
    Mocha Ice-Cream Shake, 106
    Nostalgic Creamsicle Float, 107
    Old-Fashioned Root Beer Float,
        110
    Pumpkin á la Mode, 92
Iced Cajun Coffee, 48
Iced Cardamom Café, 81
Iced Orange Pekoe Tea with
    Cinnamon & Cloves, 34
Iced Papaya Tea, 46
Iced Spiced Tea with Mint, 60
Iced tea drinks
    Banana-Chamomile Nightcap, 58
    Chocolate Chai Tea, 55
    Citrus Orange Pekoe Tea, 71
    Iced Orange Pekoe Tea with
        Cinnamon & Cloves, 34
    Iced Papaya Tea, 46
    Iced Spiced Tea with Mint, 60
    Lemon-Ginger Energizer, 59
    Pineapple with Ginger Iced Tea, 68
    Refreshing Orange Pekoe Tea, 83
    Remsen Cooler, 17
    Sparkling Chai Tea, 74
    See also Tea drinks
Iced Turkish Coffee, 63
Independence Day Lemonade, 77
Independence Day Mocktail, 78
Irish Tea, 103

Kentucky Derby Day drinks
    Cider Julep, 61
    Ginger Mint Julep, 8
    Iced Spiced Tea with Mint, 60
Key West Sunset, 48
Kir Royale, 12
Kosher Toaster, 40

Labor Day drinks
    Sparkling Rainbow Punch, 89
    Strawberry Lemonade Provincial,
        88
Lemonade
    Cranberry Collins, 80
    Remsen Cooler, 17
    Sloe Gin Fizz, 22
    Sparkling Rainbow Punch, 89
    Special St. Patrick's Punch, 56
    See also Lemonade drinks
Lemonade drinks
    Independence Day Lemonade, 77
    Nectarine Lemonade, 49
    Red Sunset, 79
    Refreshing Ginger-Mint
        Lemonade, 75
    Sparkling Pineapple Lemonade,
        67
    Strawberry Lemonade Provincial,
        88
    See also Lemonade
Lemon Cola, 67
Lemon-Ginger Energizer, 59
Lemon-lime soda
    Cherry Gimlet, 5
    Halloween Punch, 90
    Strawberry Frappé, 74
Liquid measurements, xi

Mai Tai, 13
Mango Magnificence, 68
Mango Margarita, 13
Manhattan, 14
Mardi Gras drinks
    Big Easy, 2
    New Orleans Day, 45
Margaritas
    Mango, 13
    Tropical, 24
Martini, 14
Measurements, liquid, xi
Melon Ball, 15

Melon Menagerie, 47
Memorial Day drinks
    Refreshing Ginger-Mint
        Lemonade, 75
    Torani Zombie, 76
Milk
    Banana-Almond Shake, 108
    Banana Hurricane, 52
    Butterscotch Shake, 106
    Cherry-Cheese Swirl, 66
    Chocolate-Lemon Espresso, 100
    Chocolate New York Egg Cream, 85
    Chocolate-Strawberry-Mocha
        Shake, 109
    Cold Chocolate Peppermint, 39
    Espresso Float Speical, 108
    Frozen Raspberry Heat Buster, 62
    Grasshopper, 9
    Hot Chocolate with Fresh
        Raspberries, 33
    Hot Cocoa l'Orange, 30
    Iced Cajun Coffee, 48
    Iced Turkish Coffee, 63
    Mango Margarita, 13
    Polynesian Island Coconut Coffee,
        99
    Pumpkin á la Mode, 92
    Roasted French Chicory Coffee, 96
    Strawberries & Cream, 73
    Sweet Espresso Latte, 99
    Tea au Lait, 104
    Torani Iced Classic Irish Cream, 57
    Torani Super Bowl Sundae Latte,
        42
    Torani Zombie, 76
    Vanilla Bean Café, 97
    White Christmas Hot Chocolate, 38
    White Russian, 26
Mimosa, 15
Mint
    Ginger Mint Julep, 8
    Iced Spiced Tea with Mint, 60
    Refreshing Ginger-Mint
        Lemonade, 75
    See also Créme de menthe;
        Peppermint
Mixology, x–xi
Mocha Ice-Cream Shake, 106
Monster Mango, 91
Moroccan Peppermint Tea, 54

Nectarine Lemonade, 49
New Orleans Day, 45
New Year's Eve drinks
  Appellation Concord Brut, 42
  Cold Duck, 41
  Pink Shampagne, 41
  Sparkling Shampagne, 41
Nonalcoholic champagne
  Sparkling Rainbow Punch, 89
Nonalcoholic red wine
  Sangria Touchdown Punch, 83
Nostalgic Creamsicle Float, 107

Old-Fashioned Peaches & Cream, 65
Old-Fashioned Root Beer Float, 110
Orange Candied Yam, 92
Orange Colada, 16
Orange Goblin, 91
Orange Iceberg, 51
Orange juice
  Banana-Orange Frappé, 69
  Blood & Sand, 3
  Blushing Banana, 71
  Bocci Ball, 4
  Carrot-Orange Frappé, 72
  Cider Julep, 61
  Citrus Twister, 50
  Cranberry-Vanilla Party Punch, 93
  Fuzzy Navel, 7
  Halloween Punch, 90
  Harvest Moon, 87
  Harvey Wallbanger, 11
  Key West Sunset, 48
  Melon Ball, 15
  Mimosa, 15
  Nostalgic Creamsicle Float, 107
  Orange Candied Yam, 92
  Orange Colada, 16
  Orange Goblin, 91
  Orange Iceberg, 51
  Orange Sorbet Lopez, 87
  Planter's Punch, 17
  Sangria Touchdown Punch, 83
  Screwdriver, 18
  Sidecar, 21
  Special St. Patrick's Punch, 56
  Strawberry Frappé, 74
  Survivor's Island, 47
  Torani Zombie, 76
  Tropical Freeze Lopez, 86
  Tropical Island, 51
  Zombie, 27

Orange Peel Tea, 103
Orange Soda, 65
Orange Sorbet Lopez, 87
Orchard Mélange, 66
Oriental Almond Tea, 105

Peach nectar
  Fuzzy Navel, 7
  Sex on the Beach, 19
  Sparkling Apple-Grape Juice
    Punch, 86
  Woo Woo, 26
Peach Sparkler, 53
Peppermint
  Cold Chocolate Peppermint, 39
  Moroccan Peppermint Tea, 54
  White Christmas Hot Chocolate, 38
  See also Mint
Piña Colada, 16
Pineapple-Buttermilk Glacier, 32
Pineapple-Carrot Mixer, 70
Pineapple juice
  Banana-Orange Frappé, 69
  Blarney Stone, 2
  Blood & Sand, 3
  Chi Chi, 6
  Cider Julep, 61
  Devil's Dew, 59
  Harlem Cocktail, 11
  Hot Buttered Rum, 12
  Mai Tai, 13
  Melon Menagerie, 47
  Piña Colada, 16
  Pineapple-Carrot Mixer, 70
  Pineapple Sorbet Lopez, 63
  Pink Passion Frappé, 43
  Planter's Punch, 17
  Sex on the Beach, 19
  Sparkling Pineapple Lemonade, 67
  Special St. Patrick's Punch, 56
  Torani Zombie, 76
  Tropical Dream, 52
  Tropical Freeze Lopez, 86
  Tropical Margarita, 24
  Zombie, 27
Pineapple Sorbet Lopez, 63
Pineapple with Ginger Iced Tea, 68
Pink Passion Frappé, 43
Pink Shampagne, 41
Planter's Punch, 17
Polynesian Island Coconut Coffee, 99
Pumpkin á la Mode, 92

Punches
  Cranberry-Apple Wassail, 40
  Cranberry-Vanilla Party Punch, 93
  Fancy Tropical Banana Punch, 55
  Halloween Punch, 90
  Sangria Touchdown Punch, 83
  Sparkling Apple-Grape Juice
    Punch, 86
  Sparkling Rainbow Punch, 89
  Special St. Patrick's Punch, 56
  Witches' Brew, 90

Quick Party Eggnog, 39

Rainbow Seltzer, 60
Raspberry Down Under, 53
Red Sunset, 79
Red wine, nonalcoholic
  Sangria Touchdown Punch, 83
Refreshing Ginger-Mint Lemonade,
  75
Refreshing Orange Pekoe Tea, 83
Relaxing Oriental Ginger Tea, 58
Remsen Cooler, 17
Rich & Creamy Hot Chocolate with
  Fresh Raspberries, 33
Roasted French Chicory Coffee, 96
Root Beer Float, 110
Rum & Cola, 18
Rum extract
  Coffee-Rum Soda, 84
  Hot Apple Buttered Rumless, 36
  Hot Buttered Rum, 12
  Piña Colada, 16
  Rum & Cola, 18

St. Patrick's Day drinks
  Green Leprechaun's Brew, 57
  Special St. Patrick's Punch, 56
  Torani Iced Classic Irish Cream, 57
Sangria Touchdown Punch, 83
Screwdriver, 18
Sea Breeze, 19
Seltzer
  Appellation Concord Brut, 42
  Apple Sparkler, 79
  Chocolate Chai Tea, 55
  Chocolate New York Egg Cream,
    85
  Citrus Twister, 50
  Green Leprechaun's Brew, 57
  Mango Magnificence, 68

Martini, 14
Mimosa, 15
Monster Mango, 91
Orange Goblin, 91
Orange Iceberg, 51
Peach Sparkler, 53
Rainbow Seltzer, 60
Shirley Temple, 20
Sloe Gin Fizz, 22
Sparkling Blueberry, 54
Sparkling Chai Tea, 74
Sparkling Christmas Mocktail, 38
Sparkling Pineapple Lemonade, 67
Sparkling Shampagne, 41
Sparkling Strawberry Kiwi, 44
Stars & Stripes Mocktail, 76
Stinger, 22
Tropical Margarita, 24
Sex on the Beach, 19
Shakes
    Banana-Almond Shake, 108
    Butterscotch Shake, 106
    Chocolate-Strawberry-Mocha
      Shake, 109
    Mocha Ice-Cream Shake, 106
    See also Smoothies
Sherbet
    Fancy Tropical Banana Punch, 55
    Fresh Fruit Swirl, 64
    Frozen Grapefruit Mockery, 84
    Frozen Raspberry Heat Buster, 62
    Halloween Punch, 90
    Homemade Orange Soda, 65
    Orange Goblin, 91
    Orange Iceberg, 51
    Orange Sorbet Lopez, 87
    Pineapple Sorbet Lopez, 63
    Special St. Patrick's Punch, 56
    Tropical Island, 51
    Witches' Brew, 90
Shirley Temple, 20
Siberian Sleigh Ride, 20
Sidecar, 21
Singapore Sling, 21
Sloe Gin Fizz, 22
Smoothies
    Banana-Pecan Smoothie, 82
    Cranberry & Walnut Smoothie, 93
    Tropical Fruits & Nut Smoothie, 32
    See also Shakes

Sparkling Apple-Grape Juice Punch,
    86
Sparkling Blueberry, 54
Sparkling Chai Tea, 74
Sparkling Christmas Mocktail, 38
Sparkling Cider. See Cider
Sparkling Cranberry with Lime, 35
Sparkling Pineapple Lemonade, 67
Sparkling Rainbow Punch, 89
Sparkling Shampagne, 41
Sparkling Strawberry Kiwi, 44
Spearmint Tea, 102
Special St. Patrick's Punch, 56
Stars & Stripes Mocktail, 76
Steaming Grapefruit & Spice, 31
Stinger, 22
Strawberries & Cream, 73
Strawberry Colada, 23
Strawberry Daiquiri, 23
Strawberry Frappé, 74
Strawberry Lemonade Provincial, 88
Super Bowl drinks
    Apple Ale, 43
    Torani Super Bowl Sundae Latte,
      42
Survivor's Island, 47
Sweet Espresso Latte, 99

Tamarind Cooler, 82
Tangy Orange Rind Tea, 80
Tax Day drinks
    Banana-Chamomile Nightcap, 58
    Devil's Dew, 59
    Relaxing Oriental Ginger Tea, 58
Tea drinks
    Amaretto Green Tea with Honey,
      104
    Apple-Cinnamon Tea, 105
    Apple Tea with Honey, 102
    Chamomile Nightcap, 104
    Cinnamon-Clove Tea, 101
    Ginger Tea, 101
    Irish Tea, 103
    Moroccan Peppermint Tea, 54
    Orange Peel Tea, 103
    Oriental Almond tea, 105
    Relaxing Oriental Ginger Tea, 58
    Spearmint Tea, 102
    Tangy Orange Rind Tea, 80
    See also Iced tea drinks

Tequila Sunrise, 24
Thanksgiving drinks
    Cranberry & Walnut Smoothie, 93
    Cranberry-Vanilla Party Punch, 93
    Orange Candied Yam, 92
Torani Iced Classic Irish Cream, 57
Torani Super Bowl Sunday Latte, 42
Torani Zombie, 76
Tropical Breeze, 50
Tropical Dream, 52
Tropical Freeze Lopez, 86
Tropical Fruits & Nuts Smoothie, 32
Tropical Island, 51
Tropical Margarita, 24

Valentine's Day drinks
    Acapulco Sunset, 44
    Pink Passion Frappé, 43
    Sparkling Strawberry Kiwi, 44
Vanilla Bean Café, 97
Vanilla Cola, 71
Vanilla Cream Extravaganza, 98
Veggie Mocktail, 79
Venerable Black Cow, 109
Vodka Sour, 25

Whiskey Sour, 25
White Christmas Hot Chocolate, 38
White Russian, 26
Witches' Brew, 90
Woo Woo, 26

Yogurt
    Banana-Pecan Smoothie, 82
    Banana-Pecan Tropica, 70
    Cranberry & Walnut Smoothie, 93
    Mango Margarita, 13
    Old-Fashioned Peaches & Cream,
      65
    Raspberry Down Under, 53

Zombie, 27

Also from Meadowbrook Press

✦ **_The Dinner Party Cookbook_**
Here's a cookbook that makes entertaining easy with 21 special-occasion and ethnic dinner themes. It includes ideas for invitations, decorations, table settings, music, beverages, complete menus, and easy-to-follow recipes.

✦ **_Best Party Book_**
Whether it's a birthday, an anniversary, a reunion, a holiday, a retirement, a shower, or the Super Bowl, this creative guide shows even the most inexperienced host how to throw a great party.

✦ **_Instant Parties_**
If you have tableware, music, a wee bit of know-how in the kitchen, and few this-and-thats to use for props, you can whip up any one of fifty instant parties in a matter of hours.

✦ **_Memorable Milestone Birthdays_**
Here's the only book on how to host memorable milestone birthday parties. Included are creative ideas for themes, invitations, décor, entertainment, and refreshments.

✦ **_Pick-a-Party_**
Party expert Patty Sachs has created the "bible" for party planners, including 160 party themes—more than any other book—to help readers turn holidays, birthdays, showers, and evenings with friends or family into special occasions.

**We offer many more titles written to delight, inform, and entertain.
To order books with a credit card or browse our full
selection of titles, visit our web site at:**

www.meadowbrookpress.com

or call toll-free to place an order, request a free catalog, or ask a question:

1-800-338-2232

Meadowbrook Press • 5451 Smetana Drive • Minnetonka, MN • 55343